TO REFORM THE NATION

Francis Asbury Publishing Company was founded in 1980 by several members of the Asbury community in Wilmore. Kentucky. Its aim was to meet the spiritual needs of that segment of the evangelical Christian public that is Wesleyan in outlook and to communicate the Wesleyan message to the larger Christian community.

In 1983 Francis Asbury Publishing Company became a part of Zondervan Publishing House. Its aim remains the spread of the Wesleyan message through the publication of popular. practical. and scholarly books.

FRANCIS ASBURY PRESS
Box 7
Wilmore. Kentucky 40390

TO REFORM
THE NATION

THEOLOGICAL FOUNDATIONS
OF WESLEY'S ETHICS

Leon O. Hynson

FRANCIS ASBURY PRESS
of Zondervan Publishing House
Grand Rapids. Michigan

To Reform the Nation: Theological Foundations of Wesley's Ethics
Copyright © 1984 by The Zondervan Corporation
Grand Rapids, Michigan

Francis Asbury Press is an imprint of Zondervan Publishing House
1415 Lake Drive, SE, Grand Rapids, Michigan 49506

Library of Congress Cataloging in Publication Data

Hynson, Leon O.
    To reform the nation.

    Bibliography: p.
    Includes index.
    1. Christian ethics—History—18th century. 2. Wesley, John, 1703–1791. I.
Title.
BJ1224.H85   1984   241' .047' 0924   84–19666
ISBN 0-310-75071-7

Scripture texts from the Revised Standard Version of the Bible, copyright © 1946, 1952 1971, 1973, by The Division of Christian Education, National Council of the Churches of Christ in the United States of America, are used by permission.

Scripture texts from the *Good News Bible—New Testament*, copyright © 1966, 1971, 1976, by the American Bible Society, are used by permission.

Chapter 2 was originally published in and copyrighted by *The AME Zion Quarterly Review*, vol. 89, no. 1 (Spring 1977): 24–31, and is used by permission, with minor changes.

Chapter 7 was originally published in and copyrighted by the *Wesleyan Theological Journal* 11 (Spring 1976): 49–61, and is used by permission, with minor changes.

Edited by Ben Chapman and Gerard Terpstra

Designed by Louise Bauer

Printed in the United States of America

84 85 86 87 88 89 90 / 9 8 7 6 5 4 3 2 1

CONTENTS

to
Ruth
my beloved wife
and to
Leon, Jonathan, David
our three sons

What may we reasonably believe to be God's design in raising up the Preachers called Methodists?

Not to form any new sect; but to reform the nation, particularly the Church; and to spread scriptural holiness over the land. Minutes of Several Conversations Between the Rev. Mr. Wesley and Others. *Works,* VIII: 299.

To Reform the Continent and to spread scriptural holiness over these lands. The Christmas Conference in America (1784).

FOREWORD

It is an important sign of the times that self-styled Evangelicals are turning to a critical study and reevaluation of the Wesleyan heritage (and its sources) and, at the same time, that they are committing themselves more eagerly to new dimensions of Christian social action. This is no mere coincidence, for what appears in it as "new" is actually as traditional as anything else in the Wesleyan tradition.

In the earliest and most ardent phase of the evangelical revival, John Wesley made this point about piety and social reform the focus of his preface to a special collection of *Hymns and Sacred Poems* (published by Wesley and his brother Charles in 1739). The collection as a whole mirrors their newfound understanding of justifying faith, but it also seemed important to John Wesley, at this stage, to mark off differences from the extremes of those who obscure the gospel of Christ by recourse to mysticism and those who constrict it too narrowly by a shallow fideism. This yen for third alternatives to unacceptable extremes was to remain a constant feature in Wesley's thought for the next five decades.

In his preface, Wesley stresses the vital balance between "personal" religion and "social holiness":

> Solitary religion is not found [in "the Gospel"]. "Holy solitaries" is a phrase no more consistent with the gospel than "holy adulterers." The gospel of Christ knows of no religion but social; no holiness but social holiness. "Faith working by love" is the length and breadth and depth and height of Christian perfection. . . . And in truth, whomsoever loveth his brethren, not in word only but as Christ has loved *him*, cannot but be "zealous of good works." He feels in his soul a burning, restless desire of spending and being spent for them. . . . And at all opportunities he is, like his Master, "going about doing good."

As we know, this meant that the firstfruits of *faith* are compassion for the poor, outreach to the outcast, and a healing hand to the wretched of the earth. It was a compassion born of gratitude for grace and it manifested itself in different ways and in different causes as circumstances and history unfolded. In the Wesleyan tradition, therefore, the notion of spirituality (however exalted) is never split off from the Christian reformation of society. As he says elsewhere (in *The Large Minutes*), God's special design in raising up the Methodists was not only "to spread scriptural holiness over the land" but *"to reform the nation,"* particularly, the *church*.

There is a real difficulty here. Almost from the beginning, Wesley was appealed to as an authority figure by rival partisans or else criticized for his efforts to get beyond the old rival "solutions." His efforts along this line have obscured our view of him as a theological mentor whose total viewpoint requires careful mastery and critical evaluation in the light of the norms under which he had placed himself as seen in *Scripture, Christian Antiquity, and Reason.* Anything short of such a mastery results in an unfortunate dissonance when his views are brought forward into the forum of contemporary theological and ethical debate. Such dissonances appear especially in our current debates over the specifics of Wesley's *social ethics*.

One must admit that it was Wesley himself who seemed to invite the sort of bold and easy oversimplifications that we already know too well in the massive bibliography about him. He really *was* an eclectic. He actually did read and write in haste. He was heroic in his resolve to shed the trappings of his learning and to "prefer plain truth for plain people" over speculative theology. But this has encouraged people not so "plain" to underestimate him—to ignore the breadth and depth of his theological learning, to dispense with a proper analysis of his rootage in the larger Christian tradition, and to discard his openness to the broad spectrum of doctrinal options ("opinions," he called them) in the history of Christian doctrine. Thus Wesley's heroic simplifications have too often been taken as an excuse for unheroic *over*simplifications and unwarranted fragmentations of the remarkable integration he achieved. The results of these oversimplifications appear in the current confusions among "the people called Methodists." It belies Wesley's hopeful claim that it had "pleased God to give the *Methodists* a full and clear knowledge [of *both* justification and sanctification] and the wide differences between them."

Nowhere has this tilt toward superficiality been more evident than in the area of *ethics*. The fact that Methodists who differ from each other so recklessly have all appealed to Wesley in support of their common causes should be a sufficient warning that all of us need to return to the prior questions about the theological foundations on which Wesley based his Christian agenda. This, however, calls for an unaccustomed sophistication both in Wesleyan scholarship and in contemporary ethics.

It has been a source of satisfaction and hope for me to find in Professor Hynson's essay something of this requisite mix of the scholarly competence and ethical insight that the issues deserve. Here is an edifying example of how modern historical training can make a difference in the handling of Wesley's texts and sources and in providing a fruitful analysis of his ethical theories. The axial question—old, vexed, perennial—is the mystery of divine-human interaction in the mystery of salvation. It has had various labels—"grace and free will," "law and gospel," "faith and good works," "evangelism and nurture"—but they all look backward to the original paradox of Philippians 2:12–13, namely, that we may, and must, "work out our own salvation" *because* (and *only* because) it is *God* who is already at work in us "both to will and to do of *his* good pleasure." All too often, this paradox has been recast in one sort of disjunction or another. Wesley's steadfast refusal to choose one of these traditional dichotomies has often been noted—by his partisans and critics alike—but his reasons for his rejections, and his resultant alternatives, have not been sufficiently probed and plumbed. This is what Hynson has tried to search out, with impressive results.

To begin with, Hynson has read Wesley's texts in wide enough contexts so as to identify him as a theologian with more complex and sophisticated views than the conventional stereotypes have depicted. This helps us see in Wesley's thought the links with the traditional controversies and also his efforts to transcend them. With a clearer understanding than most of the classical Protestant horror of works-righteousness, Hynson has understood, also more clearly than most, Wesley's equal horror of antinomianism. This affords a clearer view of Wesley's *ordo salutis*, with its axis of grace and its stages of repentance ("porch"), justification ("door"), and sanctification ("religion itself"). But this evangelical doctrine of salvation becomes the foundation for an evangelical ethics—namely, "saving faith energized by sanctifying love." Out of a wider acquaintance than most with deistic ethicists in the dawn of the Enlightenment (e.g., David Hume, Francis Hutcheson, Richard Price), Hynson helps us see the options between Christian and utilitarian ethics in their earlier stages of conflict. It also allows for an excursus on conscience that turns up much new material and that sparks off many refreshing insights.

A further dividend from theological scholarship of this quality appears in Hynson's convincing exhibition of Wesley's ethics as radically and consistently Trinitarian. The biblical doctrine of creation stands as basic—equally the norm of ontological goodness and of anthropological reality. The crucial metaphor here is "the image of God" as the essence of human nature and distortions of that image as the essence of human sin. This sets the premise of Wesley's soteriology; salvation is the process of the restoration of the divine image in the human creature. But this restoration is the unique work of Jesus Christ, and it therefore follows that the form and substance of Christian existence is "the new creature in Christ," understood as God's free gift of unmerited grace. This new creation, however, is begun, continued, and "finished" by the ongoing activity of the Holy Spirit, indwelling the hearts of the faithful, upbuilding the church in her unity, and holding open a redemptive future for mankind.

The result is a social ethic conceived largely in pneumatological terms. It is the Holy Spirit who activates the first stirrings of conscience. Wesley had said that it was not natural; it was more properly termed "preventing [prevenient] grace." The Holy Spirit guides the faithful along the trajectory of grace, imputing the righteousness of Christ to the repentant sinner and also imparting His character in the regeneration and sanctification of the believer (and doer). Both "inward holiness" (our love of God) and "outward holiness" (our love of neighbor) are equally gifts of the Spirit, so that one can speak of Christian ethics as the venture of *living in the Spirit*.

Wesley had made his own the Westminster Catechism's definition of "the chief end of man." He stressed the second part of the doublet with equal zest as the first: "to glorify God *and* to enjoy him forever" (beginning here and now). Thus he could link holiness and happiness as correlates. The human creature is drawn to the Creator by a divine tropism, even if also with the tragic freedom to resist and so ruin God's design. But the ethical substance of any such holiness and happiness is actually *Christian virtue* (which is to say, that remarkable cluster of virtues listed by the apostle Paul as the harvest [*karpon*] of the Spirit in Galatians 5:22). In an age when so much ethical discussion swirls around the various sunken rocks of "naturalism" (and with deontology out of fashion), it may be that the idea of an ethics of *Christian virtue* (the fruit of the *Spirit*) is one whose time has come. Such an ethic is, of course, aimed at the fullness of humanity and against all that thwarts any such fulfillment.

What we have here, then, is an admirable opening up of wider vistas for study, reflection, and ecumenical dialogue (not least of all among the separated brothers and sisters in Christ who acknowledge Wesley as their common father in God). If and when the revival of Wesley studies begins to rise to this level of critical rigor and practical fruitfulness, we may confidently expect Wesley's contributions as a theologian to be more and more adequately appreciated and appropriated—by his professed heirs, by the wider Christian community, and even by the larger human family whose holiness and happiness was always for Wesley, within the scope of God's purposes in history (cf. his sermon "On the General Spread of the Gospel").

ALBERT C. OUTLER
Professor of Theology, Emeritus
Southern Methodist University

PREFACE

In *The Large Minutes* of conversations between Mr. Wesley and others, the question was raised: "Why is it that the people under our care are no better?" The answer was that the spiritual counselors were "not more knowing and more holy." To redress the burden of limited knowledge, Wesley challenged his preachers to diligently study the Bible and the "most useful books, and that regularly and constantly," at least five hours daily. To the complaint, "But I have no taste for reading," Wesley responded: "Contract a taste for it by use, or return to your trade."[1]

I have sometimes been tempted to identify John Wesley as "the man nobody knows." While that is certainly an injustice to the diligent students and scholars of Wesleyan thought, the fact remains that too few have been led into the challenging experience of searching out the spiritual and intellectual genius of this diminutive man. Wesley founded a fellowship of Christians who have transformed the moral tone of Western society. For this he deserves recognition among the foremost exemplars of Christian faith and life. In simple fact, Wesley's life and ministry provide a model of integrity, unity, and depth of understanding that makes him an attractive source for faith and learning. As a theologian he stands tall in his development of the great issues of faith. I have come to see his system as one of the most balanced and integrated in the modern era. A Wesleyan *system?* I believe this is a correct term for describing the way he worked out his theology of salvation.

Wesley is not the most penetrating thinker in Christian history. His was not the most scientific creation of a theological organism. He was not the most careful scholar of his era. Sometimes he misread his contemporaries, but, oh, how he read! The product of his reading of a vast variety of literature— Christian literature, social, economic, political literature, the public media—was a unique blend of the abstract and the concrete. He created a system of great merit, worthy of our attention. He clearly perceived the heart and soul of biblical faith. This he joined to history—the history of his era—and fashioned a theology of faith and ethics that stands up under intensive scrutiny.

The title of this volume points up the moral and social direction to which Wesley's theological ethics moves. The Wesleyan movement was self-consciously a reform movement. When in 1745 Mr. Wesley and others in his societies conversed about the divine "design" in raising up Methodist preachers, they emphasized reform, both social and ecclesiastical, and the preaching of scriptural holiness. That simple statement of their double mission was expressed by a conjunction—reform *and* preaching. Whether Wesley intended to convey the sense of a causal relation through use of the conjunction is not clear. There is suggestion enough in his larger writings to claim that there is such a relation envisioned in the goals of Wesley and his Methodists. This means that for Wesley the doctrine of salvation, defined by the full *ordo salutis,* is a crucial foundation of his reform efforts. By reforming the nation and the church, Wesley is defining the work of the Christian ministry in effecting personal and social transformation.

Reform means that the full range of God's saving will for the world is being enfleshed in the persons and institutions of the world. *Salvation* is a comprehensive word, describing all of God's restoring work for individuals, societies, the world, and the universe. For Wesley social reform takes place in the heightened moral context wrought by God's saving work in the world. The reform of nation and church is surely borne along by the proclamation of "scriptural holiness" with all of the soteriological breadth that the term includes for Wesley.

If the doctrine of salvation is crucial to Wesley's reform efforts, it is not the only foundation. Wesley was very much aware of the Enlightenment's approach to natural law. Nevertheless, prior to any espousal of the truths of natural law, he stood squarely upon a doctrine of creation. That doctrine sharply qualifies and interprets his view of natural law, a point readily discoverable in Wesley's positions on the right of life, liberty, property, and happiness. These rights may be called natural, but for Wesley they more properly are God's gifts in creation.

This volume deals with aspects of Wesley's ethics that in

their full practical development in state and church lead surely to social transformation. In several of his writings, Wesley presents the lineaments of his ethics of reform. In his work *A Farther Appeal to Men of Reason and Religion*, he describes his conflict with the Church of England over Methodist reform efforts. He argues that his is a movement toward the reformation of mankind.

> By reformation, I mean the bringing them back . . . to the calm love of God and one another, to a uniform practice of justice, mercy, and truth. With what colour can you lay any claim to humanity, to benevolence, to public spirit, if you can once open your mouth, . . . against such a reformation as this?

Wesley then asks about the impact of his message on the lives of people:

> Are they brought to holy tempers and holy lives? This is mine, and should be your, inquiry; since on this, both social and personal happiness depend, happiness temporal and eternal.[2]

Through the intensive studies in this book, attention is focused on the developed theological and practical ethics by which Wesley's moral influence impacted the nation and church. He may be seen in the tradition of the reformers, continuing their reforming task in society. Indeed Wesley in his sermon, "The Mystery of Iniquity" gives credence to the claim that he recognized the continuity of Methodism with the earlier Reformation.

> The Reformation itself has not extended to above one third of the Western church. . . . Indeed many of the Reformers themselves complained, that "the Reformation was not carried far enough." But what did they mean? Why, that they did not sufficiently reform the *rites* and *ceremonies* of the Church. Ye fools and blind! to fix your whole attention on the circumstantials of religion! Your complaint ought to have been, the essentials of religion were not carried far enough! You ought vehemently to have insisted on an entire change of men's *tempers* and *lives* . . . .

Wesley asserts that the "whole world never did, nor can at this day, show a Christian country or city." The sermon concludes with the grand hope "that the time is at hand, when righteousness shall be as universal as unrighteousness is now."[3]

For Wesley, the Christian lifestyle leads to world involvement not withdrawal. This lifestyle is a Christian integration that accentuates the potential of Christ's Word to change the world. Never a utopian vision, Wesley's realistic union of reform and perfection offers a way of hope without "perfectionist" illusions.

To return to Mr. Wesley's advice on reading and learning, I seek to extend his challenge to spiritual and intellectual inquiry. It is my hope that this study of Wesleyan ethics may attract others to a disciplined study of one of the great spiritual leaders in the Protestant heritage. I invite the reader not to a sentimental but rather to an intellectual and spiritual journey. One of the common criticisms of Wesley is the drought one encounters in his sermons. His published sermons were occasional theological pieces, not wellsprings of instant inspiration. Like the Holy Scriptures he so diligently studied, Wesley's writings can be both highly charged with fervor and elusive to the most intensive searching. The dividends in this quest are rich and satisfying, but the indifferent reader will miss them. Charles Davis has reminded us in our own time that studying theology is different than reading the often banal literature that abounds.

> It is endemic among students to seek for quick results. They will not bother to peel the orange to get the fruit. The true value of any science cannot be appreciated without working through the difficult period of initiations. Likewise, theology must be studied for some time before it really comes to life.

Then, Davis calls to reflection

> Think, for heaven's sake, think; you are not studying a grocery list, . . . but problems that have racked the human spirit and the staggering responding message of God's love.[4]

This volume gives primary, but not exclusive attention to John Wesley. It is an interpretation of Wesleyan thought, expanding some of Wesley's conceptions to concerns the author considers particularly significant. Yet the whole treatment relies on the spirit of Wesleyan insight and could not be written apart from the backdrop of his reflection. I am confident that Mr. Wesley would have little respect for a simple parroting of his conclusions. He would not be enamored of a "school" of Wesleyan thought, I suspect. He might define "Wesleyan" in pejorative terms similar to Markus Barth's definition of a

"Barthian": "A Barthian is a reader and admirer of Karl Barth who somewhere in the course of the many volumes of his writings got stuck and stopped thinking."[5]

I owe a great debt to many persons who have supported the endeavors leading to this study in Wesleyan thought: Ruth, my wife, is my beloved companion in the journey, urging me to follow the call of my heart rather than some simpler course; Albert C. Outler, a Wesley mentor with whom I have never studied but from whom I have gained a powerful impetus to follow the difficult path of Wesley studies; a multitude of teachers: George W. Forell, my Lutheran theological advisor who encouraged careful analysis of Wesley's ethics; Joseph Artemus Byrd, a master interpreter of the Bible; L. A. Loetscher, who assisted me greatly in the discipline of reflection; Duvon Corbitt, Sr., and Cecil Hamann of Asbury College, who were bridges at a particularly important stage in my academic life.

Last, but surely first, are Percy and Florence Hynson, my parents, who gave me life and reared me in the atmosphere of spiritual commitment that I treasure above all the gifts I have received. My father has been with the Lord of the church for more than two decades—a shining light in the kingdom. Mother's light brightens the church militant in Chesapeake country.

This volume was developed during my tenure as President and Professor of Historical Theology, Evangelical School of Theology, Myerstown, Pennsylvania. My colleague Glenn Irwin was the first to encourage me to take up the task. He was joined by other colleagues who supported my sometimes arduous journey. I am grateful to all of them for their friendship. Acknowledgment and appreciation is expressed to *Drew Gateway* for the uncopyrighted material published as "Creation and Grace in Wesley's Ethics," 41:1, 2, 3 (1975–76), pp. 41–55; to *Methodist History* for uncopyrighted material published as "Christian Love: The Key to Wesley's Ethics," 14:1 (October 1975), pp. 44–55; and to *The Asbury Seminarian* for uncopyrighted material published as "Wesley: A Man for All Seasons," (Winter 1984), pp. 3–17.

In conclusion, I want to thank the skilled secretaries who worked through this task with patience and hope. Loretta Krall, Breena Krick, Juanita Patton, and Eileen Schmidt deserve special recognition.

1

A MAN FOR ALL SEASONS

The appellation "A Man for All Seasons," used to describe the genius of Sir Thomas More, aptly describes John Wesley, the leader of Methodism. Recognized universally as a skilled communicator of Christian faith and a gifted organizer of human society, he was far more. Increasingly, thoughtful interpreters are exposing the rich veins of theological ore in Wesley's sermons, letters, tracts, and journals, which were written over a sixty-year period. In the present century, a century dominated by the theological giants, Wesley's influence has increased so that it receives a hearing that could hardly have been predicted. As he experienced an increasing acceptance in his own century, so his significance has grown in ours. Any interpretation of Wesley will show his theology and life as a resource for understanding Christian faith and practice. Those who allow stereotypes of Wesley to form their assessments of him (and the stereotypes are legion) will be deprived of great insights. Wesley was preeminently a practitioner of theological synthesis he drew from the rich variety of the Christian heritage. Trained in the classical disciplines at Oxford, and drawing upon the resurgent interest in the early church that his century experienced, Wesley's mind and heart were prepared for the unique ministry he was to perform. In his reading and reflection he became a deposit of many tributaries. His primary source was the biblical tradition, especially the New Testament, and Wesley described himself as *homo unius libri*, a man of one book. Another tributary was the Western church with its static and metaphysical doctrines of sin and salvation. Augustine was the primary resource for this dimension of Wesley's development.

The Eastern church through Gregory of Nyssa provided a more dynamic theology, giving structure to a processive, spiritual doctrine of sanctification. Medieval theology contributed a mystical style, an ethics of imitation, renunciation, and surrender, especially mediated by Thomas à Kempis. The Reformation theology of *sola fide*, best expressed by Luther, was mediated to Wesley by the Moravians. In the English Reformation, Wesley discovered Thomas Cranmer and his great work on the Book of Common Prayer, the Homilies, and the Thirty-Nine Articles of the Church of England, all of which opened his mind to the church being reformed (*ecclesia reformata sed semper reformanda*). Certainly this vision contributed to his concern, often expressed, that the Methodists were raised up to reform the church and the nation.

The Arminian divergence from Dutch Calvinism entered the stream of the Anglican consciousness in subtle ways. The way from Arminius to Wesley is largely unmarked, still awaiting the research that will show its progress. Nevertheless it is evident that Arminianism received its most complete explication in the theology of Wesley. Wesley reshaped aspects of Arminian thought, asserting in his theology of sin the metaphysics of Augustine over the dynamic theology of Arminius. While Augustine defined original sin in virtually ontological terms, Arminius, resisting the terminology of "original sin" spoke of the deprivation (*privatio*) of the Holy Spirit in every descendant of Adam. Arminius was therefore more relational and dynamic in contrast to Augustine's static definitions.[1]

Pietist influences sharpened Wesley's commitment to religious toleration, which was historically rooted in his Puritan forebears. When we read his political tracts with their ringing appeals to civil and religious liberty, we are taken to an era in Wesley's own family heritage where the exile and persecution of both grandparents and great grandparents led to suffering and, in at least one instance, to premature death. Wesley's concern for liberty is derived and borrowed from diverse sources. The writings of Sebastian Castellio, redoubtable opponent of Calvin, provided impetus for Wesley's commitment to religious toleration. Daniel Neal's *History of the Puritans* written in the 1730s sensitized Wesley to the Puritan struggle, while the English Act of Toleration (1689) became the English landmark of progress in toleration. The fact that the Whig dedication to liberty found a responsive chord in Wesley may also be demonstrated.

And there is more. Increasingly, one may empathize with Albert Outler's counsel that the sources of Wesleyan theology are so diverse as to discourage all but the most determined.[2] We should not overlook the Anglican dedication to order and authority, manifest in the Homilies, and demonstrably the key to interpretations of sixteenth-century English politics, especially Elizabethan politics. The Catholic and Anglican concern for tradition is present. The Puritan passion for devotion, summed up in William Ames, William Perkins, his grandfather Samuel Annesley, and modeled in the Puritan diaries, may be recognized in Wesley's lifelong self-discipline in prayer and service. It has been suggested that the Puritan diaries were the struggles of the devout soul fixed in the script of the diary. Wesley's diary and journals were not confessions in the classical mode but they offer an exceptional insight into the spiritual pilgrimage of a complex person.

Jeremy Taylor and William Law became major influences in the young Wesley's spiritual development. Through their writings he learned that Christianity demands utmost earnestness, sincerity in intention, and purity of affection.

What estimation should be placed upon the man Wesley, the priest of the Church of England with a passion for method? He is esteemed by many in many ways: the evangelist who put his mark—God's mark—upon a nation. The genius of religious experience, who perceived the rational, emotional, volitional, and other human powers as a holistic unity. The forerunner of the theology of experience made modern by Frederick Schleiermacher, the father of modern theology. John Wesley saw most clearly the social character of the church, and this led E. Gordon Rupp to credit him with being the chief exponent of a fourth mark of the church—the church as community. Outler nominates him as the greatest Anglican theologian of his century. He was the catalyst of social reformation, whose proclamation of the worth of man in Christ took a major role in channeling the explosive revolutionary forces of his time. Wesley, the man of superlative theological gifts, wove a coherent synthesis of Christian thought without the torturous zig-zags of some of the great systems. He was the theologian of the whole church whose theology may be taken as a model for ecumenical dialogue. In the issues of faith and reason, theology and anthropology, nature and grace, faith or ethics, divine initiative and human response, freedom and responsibility, law and grace, justification and sanctification, Wesley forged a remarkably consistent theology. Thought was linked to life, resulting in a dynamic style that avoids the hardening of the arteries of classical orthodoxy, the posture of a fundamentalism that too confidently rests upon a verbalized faith as though it surely speaks the mind of God, or a liberalism that too glibly overlooks biblical faith.

Against Augustine, Wesley developed a theology of nature that avoided the negations of the flesh and the material. Contrary to Pelagius, Wesley continually asserted the need for prevenient grace. Against Luther's inability to offer an adequate experiential sequel to his doctrine of justification, Wesley proposes a strong doctrine of sanctification. A corollary to this is Wesley's balanced emphasis on good works. In contrast to Calvin, Wesley offered Arminianism on fire, calling everyone to the promise of salvation.

It is hazardous to contrast Wesley with the great theologians of his past. That is also true of the theological giants of this century. There are areas both of continuity and discontinuity between Wesley and these thinkers. Barth's opposition to natural theology would oppose Wesley's more positive correlation of natural and biblical revelation. However, Barth's increasing concern to link faith and ethics would echo the Wesleyan insistence upon the sanctification of life. Reinhold Niebuhr's realism is matched by Wesley's, but Wesley interpreted the divine agency in human experience in more positive and hopeful language. Like H. Richard Niebuhr, Wesley asserted the promise of Christ as the transformer of culture. Bultmann, as pastor, represents the Wesleyan commitment to hold the gospel free from obscurities that become needless stumbling blocks.

Theological contrasts and comparisons are infinite. They represent only a part of the justification for a careful consideration of Wesley. Beyond his theology are a multitude of perspectives that make Wesley worthy of a serious hearing. What were his great strengths? How do we account for the extraordinary success of Wesley in preaching and reform? Was he blessed with exceptional powers of communication? A commanding presence? Was he a theological giant? A superlative biblical preacher?

We may answer these questions with both yes and no. He

could communicate. He did have a "presence" when he preached. Theologically, he was a skillful thinker who walked the tightrope between God's sovereignty and man's responsibility, faith and works, salvation as both initiation and process in Christian life. He was a folk theologian who spoke to the people, the simple and the wise, the rich and the poor. As an opener of the truths of Scripture, he was competent enough to correct hundreds of problems in the King James Version (some 12,000 modifications), but to refuse to make critical study the end.[3] His effort was always toward announcing the Good News.

But if he was gifted in communication, his sermons may lull all but the most zealous to sleep. His "presence" was that of a 5' 3", 126-pound man. As a theologian he could engage in debate for pages on end, until the reader is irritated by his boring attack. He was impressed with his logical training and gifts, was dogmatic in some of his judgments, sometimes careless in his reading, caustic in certain assessments, and generally devoid of the kinds of humor we have come to require from public speakers.

Yet his speech was straightforward and understandable, his logic equal to his peers, his education superior to most, his compassion strong for those in need, his social sense developed to a high degree, his awareness of the world of man and nature continually enlarging.

In sum, he was an exceptional man, a man of God, in whom the Spirit of God was an expulsive power, whose spirit was being enlarged to meet the needs of the day. As long as he lived Wesley never stopped growing. Process, growth, maturity, perfection, completeness, are words expressing key motivations for his life. He could change his theology, his politics, his ecclesiology, if he became convinced that his positions contradicted Scripture, practice, or observed reality.

I see a number of reasons why Wesley became such an evangelist and reformer par excellence:

1. He had a superior sense of the value of the experimental method in religious life.
2. He possessed a deep understanding of human and group psychology.
3. He understood the ethical basis of human nature and human experience, appealing to conscience and will.

4. He had an advanced gift in establishing dialogue with persons of many classes.
5. He was flexible in the structural procedures and institutions he created and used.
6. He possessed an acute political and social sense.
7. He had a realistic assessment of human nature.

1. *His superior sense of the experimental method.* Wesley's powers of observation were keen. He was aware of nature as well as nature's God. He asked himself why moisture collected on carriage glass, answering that warmth from people condensed on the windows because the windows remained cooler. In 1748, he spoke concerning the effect of tea on his system, "I observed it [shaking of hand] was always worst after breakfast and that this ceased after a few days abstinence." He tested this with other people and found it held true. He advised the drinking of herb tea and using the money saved to feed or clothe the poor. He used so simple a topic to proclaim the gospel of concern for others.

In his revival effort, Wesley saw persons falling in a faint. "Enthusiasm!" screamed some of the sober gentlemen and ladies.[4] But Wesley weighed the phenomenon like a phenomenologist, like a scientist testing the consequences of chemical reactions.

The doctrine of perfection is another example. It has been demonstrated that while Wesley drew the doctrine of sanctification in its broad meaning and promise from Scripture, he based the structure of sanctification (second grace) on observed experience. The "substance" of it was biblical; the Wesleyan "structure" is experimental.[5] (Substance refers to what sanctification is; structure refers to the process of attainment.) How much this empirical approach reflected the rational spirit of the Enlightenment, or the sensationalism of John Locke (who argued that our thoughts are shaped by the senses—no innate ideas exist), or just a common-sense approach, isn't easy to assess. He was a Lockean, believing in sense experience as the basis of thought, but he stressed a faith sense that perceives the reality of the spiritual world.

2. *He understood human and group psychology.* Wesley's psychological perceptions were informed positively by Locke, and negatively by David Hume, Lord Kames, and David Hartley. Hartley had expressed a proto-Skinnerian opinion that volitions depend upon the vibrations of the brain. Thus our

actions are determined by the vibrations of brain fibers. The consequence of this, said Wesley, is to render *sin* meaningless. One man said, "I frequently feel tempers and speak many words and do many actions which I do not approve of. But I cannot avoid it. They result whether I will or not from the vibrations of my brain, together with the motions of my blood and the flow of my animal spirits." Another person compared his responses to the barking or biting of a dog. It's the dog's nature to bark and bite.[6]

Wesley recognized the importance of physiological factors and the stimulation of environmental and cultural factors. He refused to permit these arguments to be used to avoid ethical responsibility. Arguing in a Lockean manner, he declared that he had the testimony of both outward and inward senses that he is a free agent.[7]

Holding the Lockean perspective, but reconstructing it with the theological analogy of a faith sense, Wesley was able to recognize the forces that moved persons. He used this in his preaching, evoking emotional, volitional, and spiritual responses.

In his preaching he appealed to emotion, to decision, to self-examination and motivated people to climb toward Christ's call to maturity.

A cursory examination of his *Journal* shows Wesley's awareness of the mood of his hearers.

May 7, 1760	— A large, serious, congregation.
May 9, 1760	— Several were in tears.
May 12, 1760	— A civil congregation, "But there is no life in them."
May 18, 1760	— All seemed to hear with understanding. Many deeply affected.
June 1, 1760	— Some seemed cut to the heart.
June 9, 1760	— Spoke to large congregation. The "great part of them were as bullocks unaccustomed to the yoke, neither taught of God or man."[8]

3. *He understood the ethical motivations of life.* Against Francis Hutcheson he argued for the theological basis of the moral sense (conscience). As the result of prevenient grace, persons are morally aware, responsible beings.

Wesley thus asserted a strong moral foundation for life.

This moral structure has been perverted by some Wesleyans who have made Christian faith a set of moralisms. Wesley generally prevented that by his insistence upon the doctrine of *fides caritate formata* (faith active in love) and by a balance of Spirit with letter. Wesley knew that the Christian life grows not by constriction or restriction, but by spiritual nurture. He knew very well that growth is always structured but that structure alone is skeleton without flesh, blood, and breath. Expressed theologically, we need to preach law and grace.

Wesley's ethical message was as thoroughly social as it was individual. His doctrine of love is at the heart of his lifelong effort to reform the nation and the church.

4. *He had a special ability in establishing dialogue with persons of many classes.* The Revival *was* powerfully at work among the poor, yet Wesley addressed the rich and the educated. His "Earnest Appeal to Men of Reason and Religion" and "Farther Appeals" were addressed to cultured men, persons of liberal education. In these writings Wesley employs overwhelmingly logical arguments, supplemented by earnest appeals, to win a decision of the heart and will. The "Appeals" meant evangelism to the upper classes—English gentry, and intellectuals. But his special appeal was to plain men. And he really communicated. "Plain truth for plain people," was his dictum, his guiding principle. Dr. Samuel Johnson, one of the great literary figures in eighteenth-century England wrote that the clergy "in general did not preach plain enough" that the common people were "sunk in languor and lethargy" and remained unimpressed by the "polished periods and glittering sentences" that "flew over their heads."[9] It is a good principle but it isn't easy for an educated person to manage. Edwin Newman has written about the prostitution of our language.[10] Lawrence Lafore has described the impoverishment of our speech. We are "afloat on oceans of slosh" borne by "tides of piffle." But failure to communicate is a greater sin.

5. *He was flexible in the structures and institutions he created and used.* Field preaching was one of the earliest departures from tradition. Wesley adapted this mode from George Whitefield who had learned it from Howell Harris and the Welsh evangelists. Wesley scorned and repudiated canon law, which in the good name of church order fostered stagnation in the spread of the gospel. He neatly asserted that the Sermon on the Mount was one rather convincing precedent of field preaching.[11]

The formation of the Methodist societies was a resort to a familiar exercise in the English church. At the beginning of the eighteenth century, a number of religious societies had been formed for various purposes, particularly for spiritual reform as well as for spreading the message by the spoken and written word. Most prominent were the Society for the Propagation of the Gospel in Foreign Parts, founded in 1701, under whose aegis Wesley came to America in 1735, and the Society for Promoting Christian Knowledge, founded in 1698. In London alone some forty societies were meeting in 1700.

Wesley fashioned the Methodist societies to be a reforming presence within the Church of England. They were not to be considered as a "gathered church" or a church at all, since they lacked one essential ingredient of a church, the offering of the sacraments. They were conceived to bring about reform in the lives of men and women, hence in the church. Wesley's later years reveal a sharply deteriorating relationship with the Church of England. Perceiving an unfulfilled need for clergy in America, he ordained Richard Whatcoat and Thomas Vasey and sent them with Thomas Coke to minister to the Americans. This action was based upon his pragmatic reading of Scripture, influenced by Lord Peter King, that no distinction need be made between a bishop and a presbyter.

This was the symbolic act which severed Methodism from the church; further, there was the registration of his chapels under the terms of the Act of Toleration. The Act of 1689 had permitted dissenting bodies to worship legally provided that they registered with the civil authorities. After a long succession of persecutions, Wesley took the step of registering his chapels to gain protection from the mobs. The legal effect of this action was to set Methodism apart as a dissenting church. Wesley's appeal to William Wilberforce is poignant in its call for religious toleration.[12]

In summary, the ability of Mr. Wesley to take extraordinary steps in order to accomplish his mission to the whole world is recognized. He modified means to ends as long as both the means and ends were consistent with God's glory.

6. *He possessed an acute political sense.* Wesley knew what was shaping the needs and motivations of the people, their economic and social problems, their poverty, hunger, wealth, and depression. He was so much with the people that he knew more than most observers what was happening to society.

Many observers were saying there was a population decline; Wesley said there was an increase. He was correct.[13]

Wesley disclaimed any political competence or interest. Yet he continually contradicted that stance by political action, appeals to leaders, and advice to citizens. And he was frequently found in the political arena, especially during the American Revolution. This great-grandson and grandson of politically active Puritans—John White, Samuel Annesley, Bartholomew Wesley—and the son of Susanna and Samuel, who held differing political viewpoints, could hardly avoid politics. And he didn't. While avoiding the involvement of Walpole, Townshend, Grenville, and Pitt, he exerted political influence in other ways, so that many would say of him, "What right does a minister have to mix religion and politics?" Wesley would respond, "There is no holiness but social holiness. You can't be a solitary Christian!"

7. *He had a realistic assessment of human nature.* In Wesley there was a contrast with the prevailing romanticism of the earlier part of the century, with its stress on the reasonable man. During the second half of the century, the philosophers and poets began to look at the other side of human nature. But the revival touched the lives of simple people not influenced immediately by romantic visions. Life was too starkly painful for them to be romantics. The revival became the realistic, religious alternative to romantic optimism, building upon biblical themes—sin and salvation. John Walsh has written brilliantly about the evangelical revival in England.[14] Walsh suggests that in every Protestant country there are religiously minded folk who yearn for vital, experiential religion.

> In the early eighteenth-century Church of England this type of spirituality was not catered to by either of the two dominant theological systems, the Latitudinarian and the High Church, and was actively discouraged by contemporary prejudice against "enthusiasm." The sermons of the 1720s, 1740s, and 1750s are predominantly (if safely) controversial (against Deists, Papists, or Enthusiasts) or ethical (concerned with philanthropic enterprises like the charity schools) or sonorously pastoral. They offer to the layman little clear-cut, dogmatic content. They speak little to the soul concerned with the great themes of sin and salvation; they have little appreciation of the tragic element in life. There was, in short, what one might call an "ecological gap" which needed to be filled.

Wesley's theology after Aldersgate was characterized by the ultimately salvific note of a remedy for the "leprosy of sin." A "pessimism of nature," would not become the dominant Wesleyan theological stance, but an "optimism of grace."[15]

Consideration in the next chapter of the influence of Aldersgate in Wesley's personal and social ethics will demonstrate that his ministry of reform was grounded upon the transposition of ethical priorities that took place there. Years of experience and searching were encapsulated in the moment before God, "a quarter 'til nine" on the evening of May 24, 1738.

2

CHRISTIAN FAITH AND SOCIAL ETHICS
The Significance of Aldersgate

The theological pilgrimage of John Wesley provides his continuing company of fellow travelers with a fascinating example of theology as autobiography. In analyzing the relationship between his life and his theological development, we see a series of interconnecting sinews. Of particular significance for the church today is the way in which Wesley linked the theology and life of faith, justification, and sanctification together with the life of service and love to mankind. In other words, his theology and his ethics are inseparable; they are united in a precise organic relationship.

This union of theology and social ethics is demonstrated with luminous clarity in Wesley's theology of the Christian life. More precisely, an understanding of his doctrine of Christian perfection (or sanctification) brings to light the living connection between the holy life lived before God and neighbor. To Wesley, the Christian life is summed up in a convergence of the love of God and of man, loved by God. To be a Christian is to be immersed in the life of God and in the experience of man. To choose between the vertical and the horizontal dimensions (the commitment to God or man) is never an option for the Christian, for life lived for God is always an earthly life, an incarnation of God *in* the believer in the world.

Wesley was unwilling to divorce faith and ethics. His manner of working out their connection provides us with a personal existential portrait of a person who labored to realize the whole duty of man, and to flesh out this realization in human relationships. A study of Wesley's theology and ethics makes poignantly clear the early links between his catholic theology of works and his social ethics, and the later ties between an evangelical theology and ethics.

To state it differently, Wesley's social ethics was never separated from his theology of Christian perfection and sanctification. There is, however, a precise difference in the temporal priority followed in working out this relationship. It is not an oversimplification to suggest that this may be schematized into before-Aldersgate and after-Aldersgate periods. Specifically this means that after 1738, Wesley saw the relation between faith and ethics in a different way than before. Before Aldersgate, Wesley's approach was essentially catholic. After Aldersgate the relationship was perceived in an evangelical sense.

Now, lest this appear to be merely a matter of theological semantics, or an ivory tower exercise in beating the air, we must indicate the practical significance of this question. Wesley's belief prior to Aldersgate had the very practical effect of shaping his relationship to God (faith) and thus to man (social ethics). His understanding of the path by which man comes to God had its decisive impact on his personality and behavior. In particular, it had everything to do with his relationship to man, with his social ethics. After Aldersgate he understood the relationship from a new perspective. Simply expressed, this is the difference. Before Aldersgate his social ethics grew out of a deep concern to save his own soul. After Aldersgate, he was motivated by the power of a new affection and gave himself to others out of the love he came to know in Christ.

Before, he sought sanctification apart from the grace of justification. To be a Christian one strives for the holy life through prayers, fasts, pilgrimage (to Georgia), and through service to the sick, the poor, and the imprisoned. In his reading of William Law's *Serious Call to a Devout and Holy Life,* Thomas à Kempis's *Imitation of Christ,* and Jeremy Taylor's *Holy Living and Holy Dying,* he was inspired by the vision of a pure life, a life where the motivations are unmixed. To achieve such a life, one struggled up the lonely ascents to holy life.

This is, of course, a gospel of human effort. The essence of this gospel is, "You can do it if you really try." Theologically, this is Pelagianism, meaning that man by works of service is fitted for the presence of God, much as a bride beautifies herself for her wedding.

To many persons in the Wesleyan heritage the suggestion

that Wesley held Pelagian views of faith and justification is surprising. When we become aware that the essential theological climate of the church of England had been saturated with this man-oriented teaching, we understand Wesley's problem. William R. Cannon claims that the work of English Bishop George Bull in the seventeenth century so shaped the thinking of the church that human effort was conceded to be the preparation for receiving God's justifying favor.[1] It was this atmosphere of self-realization and commitment that Wesley absorbed from his early years and sought to work out, especially from 1725–38, in a sacrificial life.

The social ethics of Wesley in the period then grew out of a desire to attain salvation or holiness. His journey to Georgia was part of this effort. "I came to America to save the Indians, but, oh, who will save me?" Wesley cried out. It was the familiar pattern of these searching years, the poignant question. "What must I do to be perfect?" As the apostle Paul and Luther before him, Wesley sought for God, performing good works, disciplining self, denying the flesh, to the end that he might gain a purchase upon God.

The Holy Club at Oxford was an intensive experience in practicing the life of holiness by deeds of human kindness. Prison visitation, helping the needy, the sick, the helpless, became the pattern of Wesley's life. The Holy Club was an aggressively active association, active in study, prayer, and service.

The symbolic turning point in Wesley's social ethics was surely Aldersgate. Scholars still debate the concept of Wesley's "two conversions." Did Wesley find a relationship with Christ in 1725 as he read Thomas à Kempis, Law, Taylor, the Bible? Was Wesley following the way of faith? Or, was Aldersgate the crucial moment in time and space for this small man who became such a spiritual giant?

Each point of view has much to commend it. My viewpoint is that Aldersgate was the locus, and the moment was "about a quarter before nine," May 24, 1738. That is all very familiar to Methodists, but what is the theological and ethical rationale for the preference of 1738 over 1725? I will argue that it is Wesley's ethical conversion that occurs in 1738. From a man who sought to do good in order to win God, he becomes one whom God has won, one whose faith becomes active in love. His good works (love) did not produce faith, but faith, wrought in him by the Spirit, became fruitful in love.

An ethical conversion! This change in Wesley may be charted with a precision that his evangelical conversion may lack, at least for some interpreters. That Wesley's whole ethical emphasis was reconstructed seems very clear.

After Aldersgate, Wesley pursued the Christian task with a zeal as great as before, and with a vastly greater liberty in Christ. After Aldersgate came the revival, the ceaseless itinerancy, . . . the thousands of sermons preached to the poor and the laborers as well as the well-to-do. The common people heard him gladly. After Aldersgate came the ministry to the sick,[2] to the intellectually impoverished, to the social outcasts. After Aldersgate came the medical clinic, the electrotherapy, the support of human friendships, the exaltation of lives once held meaningless, the critique of waste, the condemnation of slavery, the letters of counsel, the touting of human rights, the doing good to all. After Aldersgate the counsel of Wesley was practiced by the counselor:

> Do all the good you can
> By all the means you can
> In all the ways you can
> In all the places you can
> To all the people you can
> As long as ever you can.

In his journal entry for Thursday, September 13, 1739, Wesley contrasted the teachings of the clergy of the Church of England with his own. He commented that he held the doctrines of the church, while many of these clergy deviated from the doctrines. He contends that the Articles of Religion, prayers, and homilies of the Reformation era represent the fundamental doctrines of the church. His response is indicative of the "ethical conversion" that has taken place. He claims the following:

> First. They [the clergy with whom he differs] speak of justification, either as the same thing with sanctification, or as something consequent upon it. I believe justification to be wholly distinct from sanctification, and necessarily antecedent to it.
>
> Secondly. They speak of our own holiness, or good works, as the cause of our justification. . . . I believe neither our own holiness nor good works are any part of the cause of our justification. . . .

Thirdly. They speak of good works as a condition of justification, necessarily previous to it. I believe no good work can be previous to justification. . . . but that we are justified . . . by faith alone, faith without works, faith (*though producing all,* yet) including no good work (emphasis mine).[3]

This quotation illustrates the theological and ethical change in Wesley's thinking. After Aldersgate he is concerned with the way faith leads to love and good works. Commenting on James 2:22, Wesley says:

Therefore faith has one energy and operation; works another; and the energy and operation of faith are before works, and *together with* them. Works do not give life to faith, but faith begets works, and then is *perfected by them.*[4]

For Wesley, faith produces love; love grows out of faith into good works. Faith is *instrumental* to love; love, good works, or holiness, is the *teleios.* We may well ask what all this means in practical terms. Wesley committed himself to social change and salvation of persons *before* Aldersgate as well as *following.* Social involvement was of crucial import to him throughout his adult life. What differences are to be perceived in his social ethics?

One difference is found at the level of primary motivation. Why did Wesley perform good works in the early years? The answer is plain. He acted out of a sense of duty and he worked out of the center of self-searching. He worked in behalf of others to save his own soul. That was what his theology had taught him. He *worked in order that God might work.*

Aldersgate reversed that relationship. When faith came he was liberated unto love. God worked in his life and the result was love, which always has both a horizontal and vertical relation. Now God worked and in consequence of new life, he (Wesley) worked toward social and personal change. He worked to save souls, meaning not only individual conversion but social transformation. As Waldo Beach expresses it, "For Wesley, it would seem clear that 'saving souls' involves personal love and social justice."[5]

This difference in motivation influences the quality and content of his ethics. Now social love is spontaneous, free, open. There is still the element of duty or ethics of obligation— deontological ethics—but it is grounded in freedom.

The force of love-impelled ethics shapes the quality of the persons and societies that are influenced. When social ethics is based on a selfish ground, the energy is diminished and there is a lack of world-transforming power. Wherever the Christian lives an authentic life, the world around is being permeated by God's presence. The conforming Christian simply parrots, or mirrors, the structures of the age. The transformed person raises the quality of life, makes social justice, equity, and integrity work. The pure in heart not only "see" God, but become the letters through which society sees Him.

Charles Wesley's hymn, "Primitive Christianity," expresses the potential in Christian love for renewal in church and society:

> Ye different sects, who all declare,
> "Lo, here is Christ!" or, "Christ is there!"
> Your stronger proofs divinely give,
> And show me where the Christians live.
>
> Your claim, alas! Ye cannot prove,
> Ye want [lack] the genuine mark of love.

Later in the hymn, Wesley writes of the divine intent for the church:

> The fulness of thy grace receive
> And simply to thy glory live;
> Strongly reflect the light divine
> And in a land of darkness shine.
> ....
> A proverb of reproach—and love.[6]

With this recognition of the conversion of Wesley's ethical priorities, from faith formed by love (the dominant medieval Roman Catholic perspective) to faith that works through love, we move to consider the Trinitarian structure of Wesleyan social ethics. Further, attention is placed on the specific problems that are addressed through an ethics of creation, redemption, and spiritual dynamic.

3

TOWARD A WESLEYAN SOCIAL ETHICS

In the two centuries since Wesley, his social ethics has been given limited consideration. Only in recent decades has attention focused on the potential that Wesley's theology of salvation and social ethics, correlated into a dynamic theological unity, brings to ethical dialogue.

It seems fair to assert that the theological ethicists have been marginally interested in the ethics of Wesley. Some suggestive inferences may be drawn from this neglect or disinterest. Those who had the most reason to search out this ethics, i.e., the Methodist family, were often preoccupied with the interior life to the neglect of the social consequences of the faith. While the science of Christian ethics is not a novel enterprise, neither is it a vintage discipline. This is especially true in Wesleyan theology for the obvious reason that it is still young among the theologies of Christendom. Yet, it is old enough to have deserved better treatment at the hands of its friends.

When the systematic theologies of the Wesleyan tradition are examined, one finds some discourse on social ethics. In Richard Watson, Thomas Ralston, John Miley, H. Orton Wiley, or Luther Lee, to name a few, there is a systematic effort to develop the moral teachings of Scripture. Luther Lee, the first constructive theologian of Wesleyan Methodism in America,[1] published his *Elements of Theology* [2] in 1856. Lee addressed the practical consequences of the biblical mandate to love one's neighbor. With frequent quotations from Richard Watson, he stressed the duties of marriage and family, civil government, human rights such as life, liberty, and property. Three sections covering forty-four pages were devoted to the condemnation of slavery. Using primarily a biblical argument, with attention to natural law ethics, Lee declared that "Slavery violates all the rights of humanity, . . . as it also intercepts every path of duty which the Creator has marked out, regarding God and man."[3]

Our task is not to analyze Lee's ethics, but to point up a Wesleyan exercise in social ethics, which the work of Ralston and Miley paralleled in nineteenth-century America, and Wiley in this century. Nevertheless, this concern for Wesleyan social ethics evident in Lee and so prominent in mid-nineteenth century America, was not poured into the genetic stream of late nineteenth-century or early twentieth-century American Methodism. On the one hand, the force of John Wesley's social ethics was diminished by a privatistic emphasis on his teaching, resulting in a graduated legalism and a sectarian spirit characterized by a mood of exile and alienation from society. This mood was all too common in the holiness movement in America in the late nineteenth and twentieth century.[4] Counteracting this was the continued spiritual dynamism of the movement.

On the other hand, there was increasing neglect of Wesley's teachings as more or less antiquarian. The increasing preoccupation of mainline Methodist thought was toward various innovative theologies nurtured in Europe and transplanted to America. The ethics of Harnack and Ritschl gained increasing ascendancy over the Wesleyan heritage. Methodists tended either to bypass their heritage or to reinterpret it in the light of new modes of thought. This is still true in certain sectors of Methodism.[5] Happily, the bicentennial of American Methodism celebrated in 1984 brought a flood of heritage materials to the attention of the Methodist churches. This means a potential renewal for Wesley's spiritual heirs.

Francis J. McConnell, late bishop of Methodism, was educated in the personalistic theology of Borden Parker Bowne at Boston University. Reared in the heritage of a pietist Methodist home, affirming the merits of his mother's sanctified faith, McConnell bore the marks of both the older and the new Methodism. This tension is reflected in both his autobiography and in a work on John Wesley.[6] His study of Wesley is important for its reinterpretation of Wesley and in its evidence of his concern to retain the values of the founder's faith.

Probably the most important scholarly perception concerning the ethical transitions in American Methodist thought is the movement from the "sinful man" of early Wesleyan thought to the "moral man" of liberal Methodist theology.[7] This transition was in some measure the consequence of continental liberal theology.

The watershed in studies of Wesleyan social ethics in this century is found in Kathleen MacArthur's work *The Economic Ethics of John Wesley*, which interpreted Wesley as giving primary support to the mercantilist theories of Adam Smith.[8] Studies at the dissertation level increased during the decade of the sixties and early seventies. Egon Gerdes, Lamar Cooper, Charles Rogers, and others have written important social ethical studies dealing with war, the relation of social and theological ethics, and prevenient grace.[9]

A resurgent Evangelicalism has begun to speak to contemporary social issues, both by establishing historical links with the older Evangelicalism and by writings that directly address those issues. In the Wesleyan heritage, Timothy L. Smith has become the primary mentor of a growing company of younger scholars. Smith's work, *Revivalism and Social Reform*, traces the lineage of a variety of reform movements, demonstrating that the spirit of the Wesleyan reformation was a significant inspiration in nineteenth century social reform. Smith is professor of American Religious History at John's Hopkins, and in more recent studies has been following the track of the Wesleyan movement back to Wesley himself.[10] Smith's first book, his Harvard dissertation, was a pioneering effort. Nearly two decades were to pass before the first signs of a small company of young evangelical Wesleyan scholars committed to the linkage of faith and social ethics began to appear.

Donald W. Dayton's recent work, *Discovering an Evangelical Heritage*[11] describes the author's discovery of the nineteenth century reform movements that belonged to his church's largely forgotten past. Defining *evangelical* in ethical and reformist terms, Dayton analyzes the antislavery crusades, the early feminist efforts, steps toward alleviation of poverty, and various critiques of an affluence that lacked a social conscience. In effect, Dayton demonstrates that the generally constricted, internalized holiness message must be enlarged. Thought patterns drawn from Fundamentalism during the era of the Fundamentalist–Modernist debates were largely alien to the holiness mentality and ethos. These ideas forced the holiness people away from their natural linkage of faith and ethics, resulting in diminished concern for social holiness.[12] While the holiness people never became Fundamentalists, because they were always oriented to ethics and a theology of experience, they absorbed tendencies with which they continue to wrestle.

Dayton's studies epitomize concerns frequently expressed by contemporary Wesleyans. Educated at both evangelical and mainline seminaries and prestigious universities,[13] they continue to build as Wesley built upon the foundation of biblical faith and authority. That is the central pillar in their epistemology. More impressed with the biblical theology movement than with the question of literary criticism, they do not reject the resources and values of biblical criticism. Rather they deny the antisupernaturalist bias that often shapes the critical method.

Grounded firmly upon Scripture and seeking the repristination of Wesleyan ethical ideals, these persons are in the vanguard of a quest for holistic faith. Having discovered the limitations of a social gospel, which was too closely linked with, and compromised by, liberal theology, these new Evangelicals propose the interaction and integration of evangelical faith *and* ethics. Whether they have learned their lessons well will be judged by future interpreters of this era.

Among other young scholars committed to Wesleyan social ethics are Ronald J. Sider, Howard Snyder, and Nancy Hardesty. Sider holds a Yale Ph.D., teaches at Eastern Baptist Seminary, and writes eloquently on the problems of violence (war) in the world, and the hunger and poverty of millions. His *Rich Christians in an Age of Hunger* [14] has received wide acclaim while pricking the conscience of many in the Wesleyan pietistic heritage. Howard Snyder has written from within the Free Methodist Church, and his book, *The Problem of Wineskins*, [15] sets forth a plea for a simple Christian lifestyle in an age of human poverty. Snyder's long term service as a missionary in Brazil doubtless has shaped his social conscience, but the most obvious influence is drawn from his reading of Wesley's theology and ethics. Until recently head of his denomination's *Light and Life Men*, an agency for evangelism, Snyder is committed to the unity of evangelism and ethics.

Hardesty taught at United Methodism's Candler School of Theology, with special emphasis on Christian feminism and the American holiness movement. A Chicago Ph.D., she has coauthored *All We're Meant to Be*,[16] which amplifies the expanding possibilities that biblical theology envisions for women.

Another person who speaks frequently and forthrightly on

social matters is David L. McKenna, president of Asbury Theological Seminary, who writes for *United Evangelical Action*, the magazine of the National Association of Evangelicals. A Free Methodist, McKenna is one of the most eloquent spokesmen of an evangelical Wesleyan ethics. And there are a number of other persons who are addressing the problems of society.

The question of their linkage with other young Evangelicals, and with the nineteenth-century evangelical movements and their exponents, is complex. One point seems to be repeated in virtually all of the contemporary effort—the influence of Wesley's social ideals. Theirs is largely an effort to revitalize the ethical commitments of their forebears. That quest seems to lead them back to Wesley. His union of revival and reform, or his way of addressing the issues of faith and ethics, has provided significant instruction for these interpreters.

The purpose of this essay may now be stated. It proposes to analyze and offer a Wesleyan way of carrying on ethical discourse. In the virtual absence of a systematic approach to Wesley's ethics, the essay assesses Wesley's sermons and writings to discover the categories upon which he built his ethical message and by which he "served the [then] present age."

METHODOLOGICAL CONSIDERATIONS

With this scholarly material at hand, what is the purpose of this essay, "Toward a Wesleyan Social Ethics"? The answer wrestles with the definition of the words used in the title, especially the word *Wesleyan*. It deals with the nature of this chapter, which is by design an exercise in constructive ethics, as the word *toward* implies. This does not mean that there is not a Wesleyan social ethics but that little has been done either to fashion it into systematic form or to develop its contemporary applications. This contention is correct whether we define *Wesleyan* in narrow or broad terms. Defined narrowly, the Wesleyan approach may mean an explication of Wesley's specific ethics, or, sociologically, may refer to that group of evangelical Christians known as the holiness movement. Broadly we refer to the development and expansion of Wesley's ideas, even the "creative misuse" of his ethics. Again, sociologically, we may be describing the whole Methodist people.

There is some ambiguity in our task. A Wesleyan social ethic is more broadly based than the narrow definition allows, while it is less general than the broad definition includes. The holiness people have not sufficiently interpreted Wesley as a theologian for the whole church. Some of them have restricted the holistic dimensions of Christian perfection not by treating it as the *central idea of Christianity*,[17] but as the single idea. The larger Wesleyan heritage for a time virtually excised the teaching and, in consequence, weakened its theological and experimental base.

A Wesleyan social ethic will not be sectarian in treating perfect love as the only necessary and important teaching, nor will it be iconoclastic in avoiding or denying its strength and significance.

Wesleyan should not be construed in exclusive terms, except for heuristic purposes. I resist the validity of the sometime "Wesleyan" opinion that the only reason for existence is the proclamation of the holiness message. Sanctification has meaning as it is fixed in the biblical *ordo salutis* (order of salvation). Removed from the context of Christian faith, repentance, justification, and regeneration, the doctrine of Christian perfection becomes damaging to faith and ethics. It cannot be uprooted from that context without becoming aberrant.

It is also important to recognize the gradual recovery of appreciation in the United Methodist Church for the concept of Christian perfection. Albert Outler has contributed to that new sensitivity. The Oxford Institute of Methodist Theological Studies met in July, 1977 to explore the theme, "Sanctification and Liberation," in the persuasion that Wesley's message has a liberating significance quite as worthy of analysis as secular sources of liberation theologies. In 1982 the Oxford Institute continued some of the concerns of the 1977 meeting. The United Methodist Church held a bicentennial consultation at Emory Univerisity in 1983 on the theme, "Wesleyan Theology and the Next Century." At least half of the seminars pondered the ethics of the Methodist heritage. Surely these are part of the Wesleyan theological enterprise.

A word concerning method is now indicated. The essay is primarily constructive, yet historical in its dependence on insights given by Wesley. It is theologically Trinitarian in its emphasis upon the social ethical significance of the Christian doctrine of Father, Son, and Spirit. It is synthetic, recognizing the need for complement, seeking to avoid a "unitarian" approach to ethics, e.g., a Christomonism. It is practical in intent, seeking to show how Wesleyan social ethics can be formative as well as exemplary. It will endeavor to show the promise of Wesleyan ethics for some of the enduring ethical problems. It is biblical in orientation, deliberately stressing the centrality of Scripture for Wesley and Wesleyans. It is experimental, traditional, and rational, but intentionally places Scripture above every alternative epistemology. Scripture does not stand on equal terms with reason or experience. It stands above, giving to reason and experience its authoritative data and their possibility for full maturity.

A WESLEYAN SOCIAL ETHICS

A Wesleyan ethics, while having its particular emphases, stands in clear continuity with the larger Christian heritage.

In its theological persuasions, it holds to the orthodoxy of the catholic heritage. Precisely Trinitarian, it stresses this in metaphysics and ethics. On a Trinitarian theology rests the Wesleyan ethics of creation, grace and salvation, spirituality and social influence.

The creative, redemptive, and spiritual aspects of the Trinity have their ethical implications. While Wesley did not develop an "orders of creation" after the fashion of Luther, his ethics was grounded in the creative acts of God. He particularly built his views on human rights—civil liberty, the rights of property, life, religious freedom—on a theology of creation. God in His creation of the natural order had bestowed benefits upon man. The Wesleyan "orders" included human society, the state, and the basic human rights.

A CREATION ETHICS

A Wesleyan social ethics will develop the meaning of the doctrine of creation with its ethical implications. It will stress human dignity by the emphasis on the *imago Dei*; the right to life, both in its physical and qualitative aspects; the right to property, with specific commitment to the right to a good and decent life, thus addressing itself to the problem of poverty; by extension of the problem of poverty and by the responsibilities of stewardship, the issue of affluence may be analyzed; the right to liberty with concern for the slaveries both real and potential, which hold persons in bondage; liberty of conscience with reference to the authority of the state or the church, the state especially, given its authority to restrain, punish, and execute, whether acting justly or unjustly. No other institution possesses that kind of power, certainly not the church.

All of these issues of human rights are integral to Wesleyan social ethics and should be amplified and applied to contemporary issues as Wesley applied them in his era.[18] Wesley affirmed human dignity, the value of life, the liberty of the individual in the civil and religious arena, the right to possess such sources of livelihood that make life meaningful. He stubbornly resisted state actions that gave legal support to slavery. He severely criticized the English state for its history of oppression toward religious dissent. For Wesley these were ethical aspects of a theology of creation.

This essay is by necessity limited to some generalizations. We may suggest brief applications of the ethical principles.

Human Dignity and the Worth of Life

Wesley held an exalted view of human life. Life is worthwhile precisely because men and women are created in the image of God. That dignity and honor is not grounded on a concept of covenant that sets certain people above others as more precious in God's sight. That is to debase the meaning of covenant and election, which involves the call to bear a special burden in history. Obedience to that call brings blessing, *to all who bear it,* Jew or Gentile.

The doctrine of human worth is not found in particular historical or racial distinctions. Wesleyans can never approve the class or race distinctions, which result in a master race, an *Herrenvolk,* whose place in history is secured by disregard of the rights of "inferiors." The Third Reich of Nazi Germany was in many ways the ultimate blasphemy of the biblical doctrine of creation. The Scripture admits of no hierarchy of worth among the various societies of the human family. A Wesleyan social ethic will not permit the distinctions of social class, race, or color to shape the Christian response to other persons. Their firm commitment to human worth leads to the conclusion that "There is neither Jew nor Greek, there is neither slave nor free, there is neither male nor female for you are all one in Christ Jesus" (Gal. 3:28 RSV). To be sure, there is a distinguishing characteristic for all who are in Christ, but it is a sign of family and service, not of superiority.

Much contemporary ethical discussion, grounded in Marx,

Freud, Skinner, or in popular art, music, and literature, treats life as subservient to political, social, or economic goals, or in merely biological or chronological terms. Wesleyan ethics does not admit that such criteria are adequate to assess the significance of life. Man—male and female—is made "a little less than God" (Ps. 8), made in His image, contingent yet creative. The reality of life lived in society—sometimes totalitarian, or democratic, or aristocratic, always flawed in a greater or lesser degree—leads us to recognize that inequities will exist.

Wesleyan ethics will function as critic of society, insisting that because God is Life Giver, no lesser power may treat human life as subordinate, using life as means to end. Further, the contemporary ease with which society treats fetal life, judging its worth by categories of physical appearance, brain waves, existence from time of conception, or less worthy criteria as parental convenience or social attitudes, will be challenged. Wesleyan ethics cannot tolerate a laissez-faire attitude toward the promised life, which is creatively realized by the responsible action of male and female. Simple answers are unworthy in this complex issue. Whatever the answers, they will respect life, potential or real. Life is God's gift, not the gift of society, the court, the legislator, or even the church. Wherever abortion is anticipated, the questions of life's value, God-given, will be asked critically.

The Quality of Life

Wesleyan ethics, recognizing the biblical orientation of Wesley's compassion for the poor, his vigorous attack against waste and conspicuous consumption, takes as a primary burden the care of those in need. Their position in society is not determinative of their worth. The theology of creation has settled that question. Now the burden falls upon those who possess more than they need to assist in easing the lives of those who lack minimal resources—food, clothing, shelter, education, spiritual guidance—to make life good. Wesley scored those who used their life and possessions as their own, in isolation from their neighbor. The genteel things, the luxuries were enjoyed at the expense of the poor. What might have fed the hungry was used for decoration, entertainment, or pleasures.[19]

Two specific ethical responses to the problem of poverty are indicated in Wesley's social ethics. One is individualistic, the other social. On the basis of Christian stewardship Wesley appeals for generosity to those in need. His sermon, "The Use of Money," includes as its third bit of counsel, "Give all you can!" The appeal of Wesley to both Christian believers and non-believers is toward concern for one's fellow human being. It is sinful for a person to be forced to search for bits of food in a dung heap while others have delicacies to eat and to waste.

Individual stewardship is limited by selfishness, lack of information, or narrow vision. Therefore, Wesley calls for a social solution. Government action may be needed to restrict waste and to provide for the needy. The state is able to control economic programs that lead to suffering for the poor. The enclosure movement was an example of a practice that the state could regulate for the benefit of those who were unable to meet their basic needs.[20]

Wesley is in the biblical prophetic tradition when he calls for resolution of the human anguish of poverty. Wesleyan ethics stands in that line, asserting that concern for the neighbor is the social mark of Christian faith. Stewards of those benefits that contribute to human dignity, Christians share them with those who are less fortunate. Neither does the Wesleyan ethic turn away from government regulation to see that justice prevails. Individual stewardship and social governance are balancing forces. Wesleyan ethics will hold a tempered view about the effectiveness of one without the other. Wesley was not starry-eyed about government altruism and beneficence, but he recognized that it could offer some solutions.[21] Doubt is also expressed concerning private benevolence even among Christians. Some issues are best cared for by personal action, while others are so massive that social action is mandatory. Government is no substitute for personal industry, but the reverse is equally true.

The Liberty of Man

Wesley's commitment to the values of humanity, life, a decent existence, and to social action to secure these, is complemented by a thoroughgoing dedication to civil and religious liberty. His zeal for civil liberty was nourished while he was young, enhanced by his understanding of his Puritan heritage. John White of Dorchester, his great-grandfather, was a founder of the Massachusetts Bay Colony. Both of his grandfathers were dissenters who were deprived of their pulpits in the aftermath of the Restoration of 1660. The note of angry criticism of both church and state is recurrent in Wesley's political tracts written during the years from 1768–1782. He attacked the kings of England, including King James I (1603–1625) for their intolerance. The Glorious Revolution (1688) was for him the peak experience in English civil liberties. It was his love of liberty that led him to oppose the American Revolution. Perceiving the Revolution of 1688 as the high-water mark of civil and religious liberty, he feared the erosion of these rights and privileges in the heat of the struggle. In the long view he was mistaken, but his basic insight was and is correct, that liberty, gained in anguish and peril, is easily lost even by those who claim to be "sons of liberty."

Wesley's concern for liberty led him to an intensive criticism of slavery, a defense of personal religious liberty and individual civil rights against the encroachments of both church and state. In each of these we perceive an ethics of creation.[22]

What can Wesleyan ethics contribute to the contemporary dialogue? It will bring its clear view of God's work in creation, setting this against shifting value norms. Our greatest peril in today's world becomes the imposition of the values of statism, secularism, or materialism as adequate moral forces to enable us to realize our dignity and worth. A theonomous ground gets us back to our "roots." Severed from God as Creator, we forfeit our history, wandering from one illusion to another, seeing reality now here, now there, and finding it only a tormenting mirage. Alongside the truth of Christian faith these changing value constructs must show their illusory character. Sinful man seeks yet another vision in place of the vision of God.

Wesleyan ethics declares that the recognition of our status as *imago Dei* means the exaltation of our moral being. We hold a clear commitment to social morality under God in our biblical theology.

Wesleyan ethics represents a clear challenge to every form of slavery in the world. Its clarion call to the responsible exercise of freedom places it among the liberating theologies of past and present. John Wesley attacked slavery as a contradiction of humanity, reason, and natural law. In his critique, he lashed out against economic, social, and legal support for slavery. Colonization based on slavery is not a source of national glory, but of shame. He appealed to the slave holder and trader and to Parliament that slavery might be finished. Wesley considered the slave as a brother even to the slavers, appealing to God's address to Cain, "The voice of thy brother's blood crieth unto me from the ground" (Gen. 4:10). By God-given human and natural right, the slave had the right to life, liberty, education, and religious and moral growth.

In a thunderous declaration, this man of typical "calm address," asserted that the state had no right whatever to pass laws that deprive a person of what *God* gave.

Wesleyan ethics, while clearly affirming the worth of the state under God, will not hesitate to appeal to the source of power—the Sovereign God—above the derived authority—to seek that justice that God embodies absolutely, Wesleyan ethics has always contained the potential for a sharp criticism of abused authority. Implicitly, at least, there is potential for civil disobedience in Wesley's ethics. There is no room for anarchy or justification of violence, but a basis for radical change in the incontestable benefit of God's gift of life.

Wesley was pragmatic concerning the existence of a particular state, insistent only that authority was God-given. He accepted the reality of the revolutionary state in which he lived and, when the American Revolution ended, accepted the American state. Others like William Law could not yield to the monarchy of revolution (William and Mary), but Wesley was not bound by the older appeals to divine right and passive obedience.[23] The central issue for Wesley was the source of power. He sanctified the sovereign God, not the contingent state.

Wesleyan ethics is seen by many to be consistently conservative, but that is half-truth. Wesley was as much liberal as conservative in politics. He sought the liberty of persons in the just state. The civil community was as significant to him as the liberty of the individual, and vice versa.

Wesleyan ethics in the nineteenth century was diverse and sometimes antithetical. Some gave obedience to state authority a priority far above that of human rights. There were Wesleyans, however, who challenged the "worst form of slavery under the sun," as Wesley portrayed American slavery. Gilbert Haven, Lucius Matlack, Orange Scott, Jesse T. Peck, B. T. Roberts, and others, resisted the evil and invoked the God of Jesus Christ who had "determined to extend to the nation the regeneration which had long been recognized as the privilege of the individual only."[24] What was this but Wesleyan ethics applied to the human values sought through the holocaust of the Civil War?

If Wesleyan ethics means taking seriously Wesley's vision of biblical ethics, some hard questions will be raised concerning the state. A stance of qualified obedience will be indicated. The state is set within the order of God, never to be idolized or credited with the authority to be master of humanity. As the "servant of God" it can hardly be "master" of its citizens. The state is *ordered under God*, but particular states neither arise as specific expressions of the divine will,[25] nor may they easily claim that their actions are in accordance with God's will. Claims of this sort must be scrutinized by the rigorous logic of Christian ethics, for this is a proximation of idolatry, putting the human order on a divine level. There are too many examples of this idolatrous aberration to dismiss the idea as extreme.

The church must always stand on guard against any movement by the state toward totalitarianism. The church in this era faces increasing danger from state regulation. If it is clearly the case that the church in the Soviet Union and China suffers under the oppressions of the state, the church in the United States faces subtle extensions of political authority. The state is not able to take the latter half of the First Amendment as seriously as it does the first. Much more peril is found in the state's tampering with the "free exercise of religion" than in the "establishment of religion."

The Wesleyan commitment to religious liberty stands as a challenge to the creeping domination of the state throughout the world. Who will call the state to an accounting? Who possesses the moral energy to criticize the state with its apparatus of restraint, punishment, its power to tax, the power of eminent domain, etc.? The church! That is the agency of reform and reconstruction. The state must be charged to establish criteria for respecting the rights of conscience and religious diversity, even when this conflicts with the political will and civil mood.[26] This conflict becomes fraught with explosive possibilities in a pluralistic society like America and much of Western Europe. Wesleyan ethics will argue diligently for the "free exercise" of religion, but never with the implication that the Christian *kerygma* is of relative merit among the religions of man.[27]

A CHRISTOLOGICAL ETHICS

A Wesleyan social ethics is decisively christological. If we discover substantial bases for an ethics of creation that emphasizes the liberal values of life and liberty, there follows the recognition of human sin. Commitment to human worth will mean concern for the restoration and maintenance of these and other values. The fact of human evil and tragedy overshadows and diminishes these benefits. Selfishness and pride turn a person inward, away from others. The experience of every man is that he seeks in pride to be as God and in consequence stands in isolation from God and man. A whole train of evil flows from that basic alienation from God.

In traditional theological terms—the Fall, original sin, depravity—the story of personal and social sin is addressed. Wesleyan theology is undeviatingly orthodox in its interpretation of this human dilemma.[28]

Reconciliation

This realistic assessment follows the clear lines of biblical faith, leading to the recognition of human impotence and the promise of a saving solution in Jesus Christ. Wesleyan theology holds a firm adherence to an ethics of salvation, to a christological basis for morality. The primary insight in this christological dimension is reconciliation—Christ restores and reconciles. The importance of this cannot be overestimated. Wesleyan ethics gives specific attention to the drive of Jesus' saving work toward the reconciliation of man with God (theological aspect of reconciliation), of man with man (social), of self with self (personal), and man with nature (cosmic).[29] Serious attention is given to the christological center of Paul's declaration in Romans 8, and Colossians 1, that there is to be a cosmic reversal of the tragedy of Genesis 3.[30] Christ is the One who restores; "Through the Son, then, God decided to bring the whole universe back to himself." (Col. 1:20 TEV). This salvific reality is the basis of an ethics of reconciliation. Wesleyan ethics can articulate a broader significance to this work by its genuine persuasion that Christ's work is for all men and the call is to all—whosoever will. This call is genuine; it is offered to *all*. The work of reconciliation is now in process and moves to the *eschaton*. Wesleyan theology affirms the process of redemptive love, which leads, as Wesley expressed it, to the "new creation." The creation—of man, beasts, earth—shall be renewed; Wesley's eschatology is filled with assurance.

The theological aspect of this restoring work of Christ presents man brought into new life in which there is a new moral relation, a redirection of moral energy, a reoriented affection. This is the ground floor of Christian ethical reflection, that the reconciliation of the person in Christ means altogether new ethical possibilities. Specifically, it is the basis of the reunion of the alienated. To discuss the ethics of creation apart from the alienation of creation is to display massive ignorance—of biblical and historical reality. The saving work of Christ is the divine resolution of the ancient impasse. Therefore, all that God gave in creation—life, liberty—is reaffirmed in Christ's death and resurrection. The atonement undergirds and exalts these values.

What does the atonement mean in the sphere of social realities and relations? The potential healing of societies through Christ's death will be recognized in Wesleyan ethics. St. Paul asserts this, showing that in Christ the dividing walls are broken down, and refusing to admit the legitimacy of any value distinction between male and female, slave or free, Jew or Gentile. (Gal. 3:28; Eph. 2:13–14). This "breaking down" is a radical reality, almost incredible except in the spirit of faith. If Christ can overcome the long alienation between Jew and Gentile, we may be assured that that power at work *through the Spirit in the church* may reconcile societies. We so easily limit Christ's work to "you and me and a few others." The death of Christ is the world-transforming power. After Christ's death and resurrection nothing has ever been the same. *Anno Domini* demarcates the new age, the "last days," the new possibility. For some persons this is a naïve, utopian dream. For Paul it is an accomplished fact—*in the Cross*, which *will* be realized in Christ's triumph. The church will participate in this work as the redemptive social presence in the world. Here we are truly imitators of Christ (a theme to be more fully developed later).

This unitive work of Christ is equally concerned with the personal and psychological. Humanity is shivered socially and personally, requiring the exercise of a precedent grace. The experience of Adam demonstrates the loss of peace, the inability to face his exposure before God and himself. The hiding Adam displays his psychological and spiritual isolation and loss of self-acceptance. Prior to their sin, Adam and Eve were naked and unashamed. The Fall shattered that simplicity of spirit. Wesleyan theology and ethics has always asserted the fact of spiritual regeneration, the healing of the divided spirit. More than a forensic justification, there is a subjective renewing, a spiritual revolution.

Finally, Wesleyan ethics enunciates the promise of cosmic reconciliation. Wesley confidently envisioned the "new creation," the ultimate overcoming of the discords of the universe. An ethics of reconciliation amplifies the Pauline affirmation of a creation groaning in travail until the sons of God are at home with the Creator.

There is a surfeit of pessimism among many Christians concerning the "present evil world." Wesleyan ethics shares in that doubt but only to a point. There is never any question that the present world is sowing the seeds of its dissolution, *but* there is a higher order under God. The Holy Spirit of God is at work in the world, moving redemptively. The kingdom of God for which we pray will overcome. *Now,* even *now,* the Spirit is breathing upon "man's disorder." We *are* moving toward the kingdom, not by natural inevitability, not by an inherent tendency to progress, not by human manipulation, but by "God's design." Cosmic reconciliation is clearly enunciated in Scripture and in the Wesleyan heritage.[31] Wesleyan ethics will seriously investigate the issues of ecology, conservation, stewardship of natural resources, and related themes. This will be our small (yet very great) part in bearing the ancient mandate to man to care for the earth. The despoiling of earth, plundering of natural resources, and waste is an extension of the old alienation between man and the earth. Without mitigating the ultimate reality of a cosmic conflagration resulting in a new heaven and earth, we must bear our present role as Christian stewards. To await the kingdom without the reverent use of the gifts that are entrusted us is to miss entirely the point of Jesus' command.

Faith That Works Through Love

The biblical grounding for Wesleyan ethics is pervasive, characterized by breadth and exegetical clarity. In his hermeneutics Wesley may sometimes appear to be a literalist. He proposed the literal interpretation as preferable but recognized that there were times when this could lead to absurdity.[32] Wesleyan theology grows out of a wide appeal to Scripture with analysis of that Word built on reason and tradition and "crowned by experience."[33] Nevertheless, there were favorite passages chosen to explicate the central soteriological affirmations. One of these is the Pauline negation of circumcision in contrast to the claim that in Christ Jesus, "What matters is faith that works through love." (Gal. 5:6 TEV). If any biblical passage may be nominated as crucial to Wesleyan ethics, this is it.

The manner in which Wesleyan ethics interprets this verse contrasts with Luther's pattern of exegesis, primarily in emphasis, surely less in fact than many have argued.[34] Their agreement on the christological center of faith and love is the central point. St. Paul's words "in Christ" are prior to the language and theology of "faith that works through love." Luther never failed to declare that "Christ alone" is the basis of faith and love.[35] Wesley's theology is informed by the same christology. While the social ethics of Wesley is articulated through the theological and existential formula, "faith working through love," it is crucial to see the priority of the "in Christ" relation.

Rooted in the saving acts of Christ—His incarnation, death, resurrection, and glory—the experience of faith is made possible to all. In the preventing grace of God (grace that precedes every human movement toward God) *every* person is able to believe, to will to do God's will, to follow after God. The preaching of the Good News awakens the aspiration for God. The preaching of the law measures these searchings, testing their character. Every person is moved by aspirations for God resulting from the prior grace of God.

Wesley asserted the christological basis of faith and linked the experience of faith to preventing grace. Faith is God's work. No possibility of faith exists prior to Christ's work. He is the author and finisher of faith. Nevertheless, His sovereign work must be received and used by man. God has willed that man shall freely believe and love Him. The divine decision, arising from His strength not His weakness, is that we accept what He gives, and exercise the gifts in the ways that grace at every point makes possible. Thus, no credit accrues to man and no loss of personhood follows. Faith alone justifies, frees, and saves; so Wesley follows Luther as Luther heeds Paul.

Wesley will amplify the consequences of faith more carefully than Luther. Luther is especially anxious about the danger of works righteousness, and rigorously argues for the *sola fide* (faith alone) position. He also insists upon the doctrine *simul justus et peccator*—the believer is *at once sinner and righteous*. John Wesley particularly worries about faith divorced from love (antinomianism). Faith alone justifies, but it also renews and sanctifies. Faith brings an actual change; love is energized by faith and grows in good works. Luther seeks to guard the doctrine of faith, without denying love. Wesley guards the doctrine of love, declaring the prior work of faith. Historically, each position has been distorted and weakened by followers of Luther or Wesley, resulting in a tendency to diminish either works of love on the one hand (Lutheran) or faith on the other (Wesleyan). In theology the adverse tendencies of a particular system, recognized and checked by the creative originators, are often twisted and undercut by the heirs of that theology. This is true of Reformed theology as much as it is of Lutheran or Wesleyan thought.

Faith energizes love and in turn is nourished by love. Love is the fruit of faith and is greater than faith. It is never separable from faith. Thus Wesley preserves the integrity of both faith and love. While describing repentance as the porch of religion and faith as the door, he describes love/holiness as religion itself.[36] Arguing that love is the end of the gospel, he will insist on the work of faith that matures in love. The "faith that works through love" is the theological formulation and foundation of Christian social ethics. "Faith alone" may be primarily personal, but "faith active in love" is intensely social. Thus Wesley, who defines holiness in terms of the perfection of love, declares: "The gospel of Christ knows of no religion but social: no holiness, but social holiness. 'Faith working by love' is the length and breadth and depth and height of Christian perfection."[37]

A Wesleyan social ethic, therefore, is first christocentric ("in Christ"), second, soteriological ("faith"), and third, social ("working through love"). Analysis of Wesley's discussion concerning social action makes this clear. Galatians 5:6 is his recurrent paradigm.

The work of Jesus Christ is the source of redemptive ethical possibility, both personal and social. Faith is a human possibility because of prior divine action (grace). Faith justifies, saves, and renews, transforming the mind and spirit, creating a moral energy. Faith eventuates in love. Love flowing from new life in Christ expresses itself in concern for the sick, poor, enslaved, and alienated. Wesleyan social ethics is an ethics of love. There *is* a strong personal basis for social ethics. However, there is the divinely ordered community of faith, a communion of the Spirit, who are a society committed to changing the world. Social reform is founded in personal faith *and* in the social force of the Christian community. Conservative Christians often divide what God has united, speaking of the priority of personal faith that leads to a reforming relationship with society. This is like the demarcation of small tributaries from the larger rivers, bays, and oceans. Wesleyan ethics will magnify the church (a company of believers) as the transformed and transforming community. As the Book of Acts makes clear, the church is a society (*koinonia*) at work in the world. Of course, the society is comprised of persons, but now persons-in-community. That makes a difference! Now one society (church) becomes the force that changes another society (world).

SPIRITUAL ETHICS

All Christian ethics must be founded upon the person and work of God—Creator, Redeemer, Spirit. Any substitution for this foundation leads to relativism and to the sure captivity of human societies by destructive idolatries. The Christian faith is being subjected to a severe critique on the question of moral values. Too often these criticisms are answered defensively. We fight the battle on grounds selected by the opponents, viewing our task as the conservation of ideals given by God long ago. Some very great truths are discovered in this stance. However, we must assert again the reality of the "living God." The significance of this reality is that values that are theocentrically based are as contemporary as tomorrow. The living God is always ahead of us working out His eternal will. We should not be bullied into believing our effort is archaic and therefore irrelevant. The concept of a "post-Christian era" makes no sense whatever if our doctrine of God is biblically sound, for God is always acting redemptively in the world.

The Holy Spirit of God is the center of this creative, ongoing divine work. Contemporary theologies speak of this in several ways. The Holy Spirit is "the real extension of the Incarnation," "the Spirit of the continued Incarnation."[38] The Spirit is "the immanence of God within His Creation, effecting the divine intention of the Father as this is expressed in creative, sustaining, and redeeming activity through the Son."[39] The Spirit is "an active . . . achieving a moral and religious object."[40]

The Holy Spirit is "God in that manner of the divine Being in which he comes closest, dwells with us, acts upon us." We "must also think of the divine Spirit in terms of God's openness, of his exigency or going out. And at once we must be struck with the fact that the language we use about the Holy

Spirit is precisely the language of 'going out,' of 'procession.' "[41]

These citations illustrate a central characteristic of the Holy Spirit. He is God's active presence in the world, bearing the power of the Christ-presence to every age. No person or personality is more contemporary and relevant than the spiritual presence. No sector of nature or of spirit is excluded from His social presence. He is the living basis and possibility for a Christian social ethic.[42] In the Holy Spirit the church becomes the social power Jesus promised it would be. Going out beyond itself the church is known in the world as "the light of the world" and "the salt of the earth." The world will know when the church becomes the social *leaven* incarnating the saving presence of Christ. A Wesleyan social ethic will find its agenda in the instruction of the Spirit and it will be relevant indeed. No responsible Wesleyan will ignore the new forms and structure of the present world. Failure to understand these will lead to a sterile and deadening insulation from the world. Nevertheless, the fullness for renewing these structures is the Holy Spirit of Christ. The indwelling Spirit is the divine provision for the world's spiritual emptiness.

In the enunciation of a "spiritual ethics" we will need to make clear the distinctive work of the Holy Spirit. The possibility of overemphasizing His role is ever present as is its minimization. Here the biblical insights and the church's traditions must guide us. The message of the New Testament is dominantly christological, but we must not mistake that message to suggest a diminution of the Father or the Spirit. There are various forms of Unitarianism that exalt the one God while denying the deity of the Son and Spirit, create a Christomonism, or teach a Unitarianism of the Spirit. None of these may be permitted because each is biblically and theologically unsound. The biblical doctrine of the Trinity expresses the ultimate wholeness and order of natural and spiritual reality. Denial of the Trinitarian position (for all of its complexity) leads to a serious evisceration of the work of God in the world. That is a point on which the New Testament is transparent.

The role of the Holy Spirit must be defined as sharply as that of the Father and Son. While the church's doctrine of *perichoresis* (which describes the interpenetration of the persons of the Trinity), is an established explication of Scripture, the Scripture also speaks of the work of the Spirit in specific personal terms. The Spirit guides, seals, sanctifies, comforts, stands by, *but never in separateness* from Father and Son. The Bible will not allow any isolationism in Trinitarian activity. The Trinity is the absolute epitome of social interaction and unity.

A social ethics based on the doctrine of the Spirit is an ethics of sanctification and of empowerment or motivation. That these are only two of many spiritual functions is obvious.

The ethics of sanctification is central to a spiritual social ethics; it develops in rather specific lines. The *Holy* Spirit sanctifies the church, the fellowship of believers. Individuals as persons-in-society (the church) experience the purifying, maturing, love-fulfilling work of the *Holy* Spirit. The social presence of the Spirit of holiness creates the church—His bride (Eph. 5). The church is becoming the community that will be without spot or wrinkle. As the holy leaven in the mass of evil, the church alters the world's program. The church in history arrests the tyranny of the Roman Empire, it overcomes the drift to national tragedy in England through the Wesleyan revival. It has not resulted in a resistless march to Utopia, as if this were to be anticipated. The sanctification of believers and the church is uneven due to human sin and failure. Nevertheless, the church is a glorious church, reflecting the divine light to the world. The prayer of Jesus for the sanctification of His people was to the end "that the world may know" and believe. The church is called to help heal the world and this is carried on through spiritual renewal of persons and the improvement of societies.

The ethics of the Spirit also amplifies the empowering presence of the Spirit. The whole field of social ethics is merely abstract theory unless an adequate resource is found for reaching its value goals. So much effort in social ethics is promising, carefully planned, correct theoretically, but without the dynamic drive that carries it off. This is the spiritual force that is given in the Holy Spirit's presence. "You shall receive the power of the Holy Spirit coming upon you" (Acts 1:8). This word of promise came to the expectant community at Pentecost. The result of this transforming presence was the emergence of a holy fellowship that went out through the earth. Before its march sinful lives were changed, and a whole constellation of social evils overcome. Pentecost was the beginning of a new community, succeeding the discords of an ancient alienation. The church brought meaning to human life, dignity to women,[43] an end to vast segments of human slavery, and amelioration of a host of social ills. Sometimes the church in certain sectors failed in its mission but the larger body maintained its search for justice and truth, drawing the rest along with it. The church today is being borne by the Spirit, carrying out its healing work in the power of the Spirit, the presence of God in the world. This transforming activity will continue until the petition, "Thy kingdom come!" is finally answered. The source of this redemptive work is not in secular, humanistic influence, or social evolution, but entirely by the sanctifying force of the Spirit in the community of the Spirit.

With this summary of Wesley's Trinitarian theology as a basis for constructing a Wesleyan ethics, our attention turns toward enlargement of the major themes. Wesley's theology of creation is filled with significant ethical content as it develops themes like creation in the image of God (*imago Dei*), persons as moral creatures, the meaning of natural law, prevenient grace and conscience, and more. The central thrust of Wesley's creation theology is affirmative of God's world. He expresses confidence in humanity's moral capacity but he never fails to see it as graced possibility. Wesley neither overlooks the Fall, nor demeans creation in his ethics. Humanity is viewed *coram Deo* (by God's standards) to be flawed, but also before Christ who has given us everything we need to conform to God's will.

4

CREATION AND GRACE

The serious and challenging task to which we commit ourselves is the examination of the worth and significance of the Wesleyan message in our time. Is there sufficient promise in the message of Wesley to challenge anyone to follow and proclaim the Wesleyan understanding of faith, life, and work, as it is drawn from the "Book of God"? Does Wesley's message proclaim the biblical content to fill the new forms that the church in its diversity is constructing today? Is the "true, the scriptural, experimental religion . . . ." that Wesley articulated in a life of ministry that touched most of his century of significant value for another, more complex, age?[1]

We seek to demonstrate the real promise that Wesley's ethics contains for the contemporary world. It is not an easy task and it is not one that will answer every question about or criticism of Wesleyan ethics. Perhaps one could do no better than cite Wesley's own "Preface to the Sermons" at the outset of this essay in order that understanding may be gained for Wesley's attitude:

> But some may say, I have mistaken the way myself, although I take it upon me to teach it to others. It is probable many will think this; and it is very possible that I have. . . . I sincerely desire to be better informed. . . . Are you persuaded you see more clearly than me? Then treat me as you would desire to be treated yourself. . . . And if I linger in the path I have been accustomed to tread. . . . labour with me a little; take me by the hand, and lead me as I am able to bear. But be not displeased if I entreat you not to beat me down in order to

quicken my pace: I can go but feeble and slowly at best; then I should not be able to go at all. May I request of you, further, not to give me hard names, in order to bring me into the right way? . . . For, how far is love, even with many wrong opinions, to be preferred before truth itself without love! We may die without the knowledge of many truths and yet be carried into Abraham's bosom. But, if we die without love, what will knowledge avail? . . . The God of love . . . prepare us for the *knowledge of all truth*, by filling our hearts *with all His love*.[2]

Our contemporary society, although removed by two centuries in time and light years in technological advance, still shares some of the spirit of the eighteenth century. Polarities exist in our world that are scarcely different in kind from the age of the Enlightenment. There are the polarities of affirmation and negation. We experience the curious paradox of an age that both affirms and denies the joys of nature. It bemoans the dissipation of a plundered earth and longs for the wonders of a primitive past when the land was fresh, unspoiled. In this we are akin to the romanticism of Rousseau whose vision of the simple life of man was powerfully attractive to Wesley and Wesley's age. Our age is caught up in an affirmation of the things that used to be: unspoiled rivers and streams, rolling hills, mighty mountains, beautiful plains, untouched by ugly smokestacks, unscarred by garish signboards, unbroken by the interlacing highways where thousands of creatures are broken along the way and where the persons who made the roads and machines are crushed by the leviathans of their own creation. Our affirmations and negations are bound up with one another. Affirming an unspoiled earth, we negate healing efforts. The unspoiled has been spoiled.

Langdon Gilkey has stressed the fact that contemporary humanity is alienated from the cosmos, from people, plants, animals, and landscapes. Basic to this alienation, says Gilkey, are the

> . . . eradication of teleology, valuation, and "meaning" from the processes of nature; the spiritual or existential separation of man from both the beauty and the awe of surrounding nature which technology and urbanization have gradually effected; and, finally the gradual loss, culminating in the twentieth century, of a sense of an ultimate or directedness in the process of things.[3]

It is strange that an age that so vigorously emphasizes natural ecology should be so self-destructive in its manipulations of human ecology. Many persons who so fervently desire communion with the earth and the world of nature demonstrate a tragically twisted perception, void of proper acceptance and use of that which nature yields. Still it is an age of profound interest in nature, as was Wesley's world.

Ours is a world in which the polarities of order and disorder prevail. So was Wesley's. It is an era of rationalism and of irrationalism. So much of life today consists of an attempt to touch the depths, the ground of the human spirit, the inarticulate, subconscious, formless. The primitive earth of Genesis 1, which is described as *tohu-wabohu*, without form and void, is an apt picture of the contemporary human spirit in its perception of its own essence and destiny. Increasingly complex in these days is the communication and reinforcement of treasured values to a younger generation attuned to the affective more than the rational. Even student theologians are with difficulty convinced of the significance of wrestling with the church's doctrinal treasures and their use as currency in today's world.

Wesley's century, like this one, was preoccupied with nature, and sometimes with nature's God, although too often He seemed a hidden God. Bishop Francis J. McConnell has stated:

> The Deists . . . said there was no news from God; the more stern Calvinists made the gospel bad news, except for themselves. It was the task of Wesley to convince the masses of his time that there was at hand news from God and that news was good.[4]

The Wesley scholar, William R. Cannon, has stressed that in an age where the Copernican revolution had altered the view of man and earth, Wesley maintained both an affirmative view of the created world and of man in God's world. Of primary interest to Wesley, Cannon writes, was humanity's significance in terms of its place, not in the intellectual or physical order, but in the spiritual order.[5] While this seems to be correct, it would be a serious mistake to deemphasize the Wesleyan affirmation of the natural world and of man in that world.

A primary concern in present biblical interpretation is fidelity to the various forms of biblical theology. Walter Brueggemann has spelled this out in a superb discussion.[6] He asserts that biblical theologians have long stressed salvation history, as virtually the only important theology of Scripture. Brueggemann has worked extensively in biblical theology[7] and concludes that there are four important theological emphases in Scripture:

1. *Theology of creation*—stressing our strength, ability, resourcefulness, as God's creatures. Emphasizes wholeness of man's being, the integrated person. Teaches man's ability and responsibility.
2. *Theology of salvation*—emphasizing our helplessness, depravity, alienation from God and the world. We need a Savior from the sins that erode and destroy our being.
3. *Wisdom theology*—amplifying our intellectual powers, our capacities for moral perception and discrimination. Involves the serious "theological effort to talk faith with sense."
4. *Royal theology*—emphasizing that the initiative and responsibility for shaping human life is in human hands, the deliberate and willing gift to God.

This effort by Brueggemann points up the significant concern in our era for an adequate theology of creation, a more balanced interpretation of the totality of the Word than that which centers attention upon the saving acts of God. We cannot wish to lessen our concentration upon salvation in Scripture, but to assert the essential principle of fidelity to the message of the *total* biblical canon. I wish to assert that Wesley's theological ethics speaks pertinently to this discussion.

Following this general introduction to our problem, we may now venture upon an examination of Wesley's understanding of the issues of creation and grace. What is Wesley's view of creation and the Creator and how is this perceived in his personal and social ethics? Further, what is the relationship of grace to creation? Does grace hold a relationship of complementarity to nature? Did Wesley submerge his theology of creation beneath his doctrines of grace? What is the significance of the *imago Dei*, the image of God, in Wesley's personal, social, or political ethics? What does the *imago Dei* mean in ethical terms?

Wesley lived at the center of the Enlightenment, which so significantly shaped the course of Western thought. In philosophy, John Locke's stress upon sensation as the source of knowledge of the world was central to the development of empiricism, which, radicalized, becomes problematic for biblical faith. Immanuel Kant taught in his concepts of pure and practical reason the idea that although God could not be known by the usual criteria of reason, there was the knowledge of God "in the starry sky above and the moral law within," a philosophical mirror of the orthodox view of the world as the "theater of the divine glory." The Deist, Matthew Tindal, wrote his *Christianity as Old as Creation* in 1730, a reductionist work indicating that no difference can be made between faith and reason, that in fact faith *is* reason. The result was the perception of Christianity as a continuum of religion from the creation until his day. Classical deism, of course, negated the idea of a living, active Lord of history.

John Wesley received, assimilated, and shaped from his sources in the Scriptures and from his keen observations of nature a theology of creation that, like the theologies of Calvin and Luther, envisioned the Creator in a sustaining, integral relationship to the world he had formed. His perception of creation was thoroughly biblical but it was also informed by his reading of the natural philosophers (physicists, astronomers) of his time. He adapted their ideas to his biblical viewpoint and brought them together in his edited work, *A Survey of the Wisdom of God in the Creation.*

GOD THE CREATOR

In Wesley's theology God has revealed Himself to man as Creator and as Governor. As Creator He acted sovereignly, doing what His wisdom and good pleasure indicated. He created when He wanted to; there is no need to ask the question of the timing of God's acts. God determined the length of time, appointed the universe its place, and set the stars in their courses.[8] He gave to the material and the vital their form and properties. Having scrutinized the whole He pronounced it good, that is, a mirror of His own perfection. Everything was integrated, characterized by wholeness: "But when He saw everything He had made, *all in connexion* with each other. . . ."[9]

The creation is characterized by purpose, giving evidence of an intelligent cause acting freely and not capriciously. Such is His goodness that His power is shaped to the advantage of His creatures,[10] yet justice and holiness prevent Him from a subservience to His creatures, which would mean the end of creation and a return to chaos. His creature, man, is like Himself, endued with understanding, will, and liberty.

What kind of world is this that God has created out of nothing? It is all good, and this means that nothing that He made is evil. It is expressive of His will and directs us to Him. Wesley likens the world about us to a massive volume that proclaims God to us not in words, but in pictures of the divine. These are only analogies of the Creator, finite, yet they provide glimmerings of Him.[11]

The sky suggests immensity, the storm His wrath. Rain and sunshine bespeak His munificence, and perpetual renewal of life is an intimation of His eternity. The vast forms of life imply the infinity of His diffuse life and power, while death suggests the "infinite disproportion between Him and all living things." So Wesley concludes "that every part of nature directs us to nature's God."[12]

The immensity of creation and the vast diversity of the creatures reflect God's might and sing praises to Him. Creation began with four simple elements: earth, air, fire, and water, and these were expanded by the Creator into compound bodies. Both animate and inanimate existences were created by God to fulfill their end in creation that all of them together might form a marvelous mosaic of living forms, exhibiting the complementary wholeness of creation. Wesley's figure, borrowed from Plato, was that of a golden chain let down from heaven. He wrote:

> Such was the state of the creation, . . . when its great author, surveying the whole system at one view called it "very good." It was good in the highest degree whereof it was capable and without any mixture of evil. Every part was exactly suited to the others, and conducive to the good of the whole. There was a "golden chain" . . . an exactly connected series of beings from the highest to the lowest, from dead earth, through fossils, vegetables, animals, to man, created in the image of God, and designed to know, to love, and enjoy this Creator to all eternity.[13]

The same idea of the interconnection of all life-forms in ascending gradation is stressed by Wesley in *A Survey of the Wisdom of God in Creation*:

> The whole progress of nature is so gradual, that the entire chasm from a plant to a man, is filled up with diverse kinds of creatures, rising one above another, by so gentle an ascent, that the transitions from one species to another are almost insensible. And the intermediate space is so well

husbanded, that there is scarce a degree of perfection which does not appear to some. Now since the scale of being advances by such regular steps as high as men, is it not probable, that it still proceeds gradually upwards, through beings of a superior nature? As there is an infinitely greater space between the Supreme Being and man, than between man and the lowest insect.[14]

This commentary by Wesley is an abridgment of the work of Charles Bonnet's *The Contemplation of Nature*, from whom he quoted twelve chapters totaling more than 150 pages. Born in 1720 of wealthy French Huguenot parents, Bonnet became a leading biologist, thoroughly Christian, convinced of the wisdom of God in the creation. He stressed particularly the progressive development going on in nature. An optimist, he believed that nature is advancing towards a high goal. He maintained that nature draws no sharply defined lines between the species, a notion seen in Wesley's statement above.[15]

Robert Andrews Millikan, the 1923 Nobel Prize winner for physics, saw Wesley to be something of an evolutionist, on the basis of his reading of Wesley's abridgment of Bonnet.[16] However, the clear intention of Wesley is to extol the glories of the Creator and to demonstrate the marvelous order of His creation. The Wesleyan view of this world is affirmative, not distorted by religious or scientific dogmatism. It avoids materialism, radical transcendence or immanence, pantheism, and irrationalism. Wesley here demonstrates that he is a man of reason, a true man of the Enlightenment, who refused to denigrate reason, but who also resisted its elevation to a position of solitary sovereignty in the process of knowing. The creation marvelously demonstrates the order of the divine mind. The mind of man is a mirror of the divine.

Wesley's sermon, "God's Approbation of His Works," was written to challenge the ascription of finitude or limitation of God. Any defects in the creation were imposed upon it subsequently by man's apostasy, which "threw not only man himself, but likewise the whole creation, which was intimately connected with him, into disorder, misery and death. . . ."[17] Evil does not emerge because of some inherent flaw in God or His works, but in our fateful abuse of the liberty God gave us. That liberty was perfect. To be perfect it must be possible for us to shape it in the ways the human spirit should choose. (Wesley is careful to insist, against Gnosticism, that matter is not essentially evil in itself.) By not depriving man of liberty, God permitted the possibility that man might become an alien to his Creator, but also provided the possibility of cheerful and devout service.

The world *has* been overspread with a "whole army of evils," Wesley asserts, which grind the creation under their destructive advance. Nevertheless, the whole creation—torn, groaning, and spoiled—awaits the Day of the Lord. It comes, Wesley announces. Even in the midst of a world that is filled with savagery and cruelty, the perverse arts in which man so excels, the *whole* creation will experience a restoration.[18] Creation in all its forms will regain its ancient beauty, and its exaltation will exceed the glory of the remembered Paradise. In a thoroughly biblical vein, Wesley decisively implies that the present creation, however broken, is God's ancient master-piece, the amphitheater upon which mankind fights its painful but ultimately triumphant battle against sin and death. God is working now through His Son and through a redeemed community, the church, calling her to wrest the whole creation from Satan's grasp. As Wesley notes in his comment on Revelation 11:15, "The kingdom of this world is become the kingdom of our Lord. . . ." This province has been in the enemy's hands; it now returns to the rightful master. In reality, all things (and so the kingdom of the world) are God's in all ages: . . . God now puts an end to this monstrous rebellion.[19] God has no intention of yielding up any part of His creation to the rebel. Thus Wesley declares the triumph of the divine will.

DIVINE GOVERNMENT

To further stress the ceaseless love of God for His whole creation, Wesley asserts a concept of God's presence and providence that is strikingly modern in its note, similar to the processive emphases of Whitehead and his interpreters, and to Teilhard de Chardin. Not pretending that man can understand the manner by which God pervades and sustains His whole creation, he insists that God knows every connection and relation in His world.

> As certain as it is, that he created all things, and that he *still sustains all that is created;* so certain it is, that he is present, at all times, in all places. . . . Perhaps what the ancient philosopher speaks of the soul, in regard to its residence in the body . . . might be spoken of the omnipresent Spirit, in

regard to the universe: that he is not only, "All in the whole," but "All in every part."[20]

Again he argues that "every point of infinite space is full of God."[21] That God continues every moment to infuse the whole creation with His sustaining presence seems to contradict the suggestion made by some Christian pacifists that the world, and especially the governments of man, have been seized by Satan and are now under his control.

MAN

The exaltation of man is an integral part of Wesley's theology and ethics of creation. When judged in terms of magnitude or duration, man is as a grain of sand in contrast to God's universe. Measured by God's order, humanity participates in the glories of God Himself.

> Man is not only a house of clay, but an immortal spirit; a spirit made in the image of God an incorruptible picture of the God of glory; a spirit that is of infinitely more value than the whole earth; of more value than the sun, moon, and stars, put together; yea, than the whole material creation. Consider that the spirit of man is . . . of a higher order, . . . than any part of the visible world.[22]

"What is man?" Wesley asked. A complex composition of earth, air, fire, and water. Beyond this, man is a creature of thought, imagination, and memory. Perceiving objects by the senses, man forms inner ideas (here Wesley follows Locke). Judgments are made concerning these ideas and reasoning or reflection is carried on. This "thinking principle," as Wesley describes it, is an aspect of that "inward principle" called the soul. Body and soul are now so intimately connected that Wesley extrapolates the eternal union of both body and soul. If the soul, so much a present expression of man, is to continue to exist, then who should doubt that the body will share that future relation? "In my present state of existence, I undoubtedly consist both of soul and body: And so I shall again, after the resurrection, to all eternity."[23]

What is man? He is characterized by liberty or the power of self-determination. In the order of nature man is free to make many choices. In the order of grace, man is free to choose good, assisted by God's grace.

Man is created in the image of God; that is his greatest

glory. Bearing the natural image of God, we mirror the intelligence, liberty, and majesty of God. The moral image of God is evidenced in man's original holiness and wholeness, and, although sorely defaced in human personality, it is still God's purpose for persons destined in Christ to fully bear again the character of love. Like the sovereign God, man possesses the special dignity and honor of derived sovereignty, evidenced in his call to keep the Garden and to have dominion over the creatures. Wesley sees the rulership of man over other persons as one of the highest expressions of our participation in the image of the divine authority. The ultimate tragedy of the universe was inaugurated in the rebellion of man.

THE GOD OF GRACE

When humanity broke the relationship between itself and the Creator, it was plunged into a chasm of profound and hopeless alienation. It was here that God initiated what He had purposed from the foundations of the world. Here the grace of God operated, especially the grace that is designated by Wesley as prevenient grace, the grace that precedes man's ability to act and has reference to God's grace in salvation. Wesley's ethics is here set within a theology of grace, not a theology of creation.

It is important to indicate the significance for Wesleyan ethics of this concept of prevenient grace. *Ethics is grounded in the grace of God. Because of prevenient grace, everyone is capable of moral action, and is morally responsible. Morality is an intimate expression and consequence of grace.* Conscience is a reflection of the power of prevenient grace, a means by which God in a *preliminary* way makes Himself known and by which are pointed out in a *general* way the "lines of good and evil."[24] Conscience then, as well as faith, is a gift of grace.

Prevenient grace makes freedom of choice possible and opens to us the potential for becoming what we were originally meant to be. Through grace man can work with God to receive what God offers. And we must work.[25]

It can be argued that, because there is no one who is in a "state of mere nature," no one who is void of God's grace, no one without conscience except for a few incorrigibles, Wesley's theology sees man as capable of a greater degree of moral potential than some theologies permit. This allows man to be more truly and completely human. In a word, Wesleyan ethics appears to make possible a more positive humanizing than many have recognized. (Thus it is sometimes categorized as Pelagian.) We are more human because we are more truly responsible. Prevenient grace renews again in man the powers of understanding, volition, and liberty in the order of salvation.

Prevenient grace is important in respect to salvation and the moral life in the experience of those who have never been introduced to Jesus Christ, but "who having not the law, do by nature the things contained in the law. . . . Who show the work of the law written upon their hearts, their conscience also bearing witness, and their thoughts among themselves accusing or even defending *them;* in the day when God will judge the secrets of men by Jesus Christ." This is Wesley's translation of Romans 2:14–16, an important biblical teaching on the operation of prevenient grace in the experience of man in the non-Christian world.

Wesley makes several important points regarding Paul's discussion. First, these verses refer to Gentiles, or heathen, not Jews. Second, he sees Paul making some kind of concession to these heathen. Third, he indicates that when heathen "do by nature the things contained in the law," they do so by prevenient grace. Fourth, the Decalogue is only the substance of the law of nature. By "substance" Wesley evidently means the essence of the law of nature. Fifth, since these heathen do not have the written law, they themselves, "by the grace of God," are a law to themselves, a rule of life. Conscience fills the place of the written law for such persons. "Conscience and sin itself are witnesses against the heathen. *Their thoughts* sometimes excuse, sometimes condemn them. . . . *Accusing or even defending them—* . . . they have far more room to accuse than to defend." Sixth, Wesley stresses in the *Notes* that verse 16, concerning the judgment of man's secrets by Jesus Christ, depends on verse 15, not verse 12, intimating that there is specific reference to the judgment of those who have not the written law but who have the law of nature written on the heart. This concerns the judgment of the heathen when the law written on their hearts will either accuse or defend. Wesley may indeed be implying that in responding to prevenient grace these persons, like the patriarchs of old, may be justified by faith in anticipation of Christ's ultimate self-disclosure to them.[26] Does this concept undercut the Christian mission to the world? No! It does magnify God's grace and love for all. The history of salvation is operative in the whole world. God wills that all men share its treasures in this life, so that man may consciously, willingly, joyfully share in God's life even now. Ethically, this suggests a different quality of morality in the life of the "honest heathen" because of the operation of grace in his life.

NATURAL MAN

A facet of Wesley's thought particularly crucial for his ethics is the concept of the "law of nature." What is this law, and to whom was it given? When God the Creator fashioned the angels, "his firstborn sons," He made them creatures of understanding and liberty and gave them a law that challenged these capacities. It was a "complete model of all truth," and all good. God "created a new order of intelligent beings," man, and wrote upon his heart the same law. God meant this law never to be far away from man, never difficult to understand. This law was coeval (of the same age—contemporary) with man's nature, or inseparable from human nature. *It is the moral law.*

This law is the unblemished picture of God, "the face of God unveiled," the "heart of God disclosed to man." The law of God is all virtues in one, Wesley asserts. Using Platonic categories and transvaluating them, he indicates that the law is

> divine virtue and wisdom assuming a visible form. What is it but the original ideas of truth and good which were lodged in the uncreated mind from eternity, now drawn forth and clothed with such a vehicle as to appear even to human understanding?

Wesley calls the moral law "unchangeable reason; it is unalterable rectitude, it is the *everlasting fitness of all things that are or ever were CREATED.*" This law is a "copy of the eternal mind, a transcript of the divine nature."[27]

What is Wesley arguing in this sermon on the law? In what Edward Long calls a "deliberative" approach[28] or an ethics of natural law, Wesley is stressing the changeless character of moral law. There is in God's creation an established moral order, a fixed rectitude in the relationships that God made. The law is holy, just, and good for it is the "transcript of the divine mirror" that displays the character of man's deeds, including the alteration or breaking of the divine order that God established for the regulation of man's relationships. The things that God created comprise a consistent and coherent whole.

Each part is integral to the whole and possesses its own separate worth. The law is just. "It is adapted in all circumstances of each. . . . If the law, the immutable rule of right and wrong, depends upon the nature and fitnesses of things, and on their essential relations with each other . . . then it must depend on God, . . . because those things themselves, with all their relations, are the work of His hands."[29]

Wesley's ethics here takes shape in his theology of creation as well as his theology of salvation. Ethics, the wrestling with issues of right and wrong in the moral life, interprets man's experiences (actions, thoughts, intentions) by the law of nature, which is a copy of the divine perfection. Whenever man alters that ultimate criterion, his sin weakens and violates the order of the created world and shifts the balance of relationships.

When man rebelled against God, there was set in motion a pattern of discontinuity whereby right relationships were confounded. Man, made to have dominion over the creatures and to be their lord, became brutish, exercising the cunning of the wilds, destroying without concern the life of creatures. The lion, tiger, and shark cause pain in order to survive, but the "human shark" torments without reason. And so the whole creation groans together in one vast litany until the new creation comes.[30]

Yet, despite the fact that the law was nearly effaced in man by the Fall, God "in some measure, reinscribed the law on the heart of his dark, sinful creature," through His prevenient grace. Thus, the law of God, the moral law, a concomitant of human nature, *first by creation* and *then by grace*, remains as the standard of human relationships, prescribing what is right with regard to God, to ourselves, and to all of God's creatures.

How did Wesley apply this concept of moral law, or the law of nature, in his ethical judgments? We note his appeal to moral law and its significance in the sphere of human liberty. He made crystal clear his conviction that God has ordered the human situation so that every man possesses religious liberty, the right to worship God according to the demands of conscience.

> Every man living, as man, has a right to this, as he is a rational creature. The Creator gave him this right when he endowed him with understanding. And every man must judge for himself, because every man must give an account . . . to God. Consequently, this is inseparable from humani-

ty. And God never did give authority to any man, or number of men, to deprive any child of man thereof, under any cloud or pretence whatever.[31]

This is a liberty that is "a kind of natural instinct antecedent to art or education." A parallel of religious liberty is civil liberty, which is the right to enjoy life, person, and property that is legally ours, according to our own choice. Never is Wesley's commitment to the justice that moral law demands more patent than in his polemic against slavery. Arguing that God intended no one to live as slaves are forced to live, Wesley resisted the appeal to human law as justification for slavery. He asked:

> But can law, human law, change the nature of things? Can it turn darkness into light, or evil into good? By no means. Not withstanding ten thousand laws, right is right, and wrong is wrong still. . . . So that I still ask, who can reconcile this treatment of the Negroes, first and last, with either mercy or justice? Slavery is utterly inconsistent with any degree of natural justice. Unlike ownership in sheep, no one should ever be born a slave. "Liberty is the right of every human creature, as soon as he breathes the vital air, and no human law can deprive him of that right which he derives from the law of nature." The slave is the brother of the slave owner or trader and should be respected as such.[32]

GRACE AND RECONCILIATION

The ethical possibilities for humanity after the Fall were sharply changed. The power to understand and to do God's will was forfeited and lost. Man could not carry on the reflective processes by which right or wrong may be discerned. However, humanity was not left in its fallen, natural state, untouched by the divine mind and will. By the prevenient grace of God, humanity was assisted toward contrition, decision, and faith. This became effectual through the work of Jesus Christ, through whom grace and truth were brought to mankind (John 1:17).

Christian ethics for Wesley is the reaffirmation of creation ethics. While creation began with the divine initiative which brought the raw material of the universe into existence and shaped it into glorious order, the saving process of God in Christ begins with a different datum. Now rebellious, discordant, and lost, humanity requires another act of God. Here grace reaches its apex. In Christ we see the "exceeding kindness of God's grace" (Eph. 2:7). "Grace," declared Wesley, "without any respect to human worthiness, confers the glorious gift. Faith, with an empty hand, and without any pretense to personal desert, receives the heavenly blessing."[33] The saving acts of God are consummated in the incarnation, death, and resurrection of Jesus the Christ. Whether with creation or salvation, the initiative belongs to God. Wesley affirmed the continuing moral and spiritual obligation to God which grace renews and sustains.

The major ethical implications of Wesley's doctrine of salvation by grace may be summed up in terms of restoration and reconciliation. The apostle Paul's description of the death of Christ as a reconciling work is woven into the church's theology of the atonement. Irenaeus and Anselm are two of many Christian thinkers who taught the unitive significance of Christ's suffering and death at Calvary. Wesley's doctrine of grace draws upon the concepts of Anselm which focused on propitiation, or the belief that Christ's death offered objective satisfaction for the sins of humanity. Beyond that emphasis, Wesley incorporates the teaching of Irenaeus known as recapitulation: "When he [Christ] was incarnate and became man, he recapitulated in himself all generations of mankind, making himself the centre of our salvation, that what we lost in Adam, even the image and likeness of God, we might receive in Jesus Christ."[34] When Jesus Christ joined himself to the human race in life and death, he forever changed its possibilities. One with us in the full range of our experience, he died and was raised again to bring us to fellowship with the Father.

The ethical meaning of restoration and reconciliation is evident. As the apostle Paul states, we are "buried with him by baptism into death." Because of this we are enabled to walk with Christ in "newness of life" (Rom. 6:4; 2 Cor. 5:14–15). We are *enabled* and *obligated*! Wesley continually affirms this in his familiar use of the theological concepts of regeneration and sanctification.

Reconciliation, according to the theology of Paul, conveys the "in Christ" prospect of the restoration of all broken relationships. "In Christ" both Jew and Greek, man and woman, slave and free, are one. "In Christ" the walls are taken down and the hostility is overcome. "In Christ" the whole creation drives toward overcoming all the anguish and discord which is recorded in the long history of the world (Rom. 8:18–

27; Gal. 3:28; Eph. 2:11–18). In Wesleyan theology this is known as "The Great Deliverance." The substratum for such a restoration is grace alone, *sola gratia*.

CONCLUSION

The conclusions that seem to flow from this analysis of Wesley's ethics are important. In the preaching of the *kerygma* with its ethical implications, Wesley's message becomes alive for us today.

First, we may assert the essential value of this natural order or creation with the perfection it bears as the work of God. We do not need to move through this world in numbing fear of the material. Wesley affirmed God's world without naïvely overlooking the recurrent presence of tragedy and sinfulness. The earth is the Lord's and His presence fills it, sustains it, and is redeeming it. In the perpetuation of the Wesleyan message, we have sometimes tended toward negation more than affirmation. Our articulation of the message of Christian perfection has too often sounded more like the austere Wesley of the pre-Aldersgate years than the apostle of Christian freedom in love. We have wrongly associated holiness with isolation or retreat. Yet our conscience suffers disquiet because we have never been able to reconcile retreat with the claims of the Christian gospel. Let us now seek to affirm all that God has created and all that He continuously infuses with His presence. He shall ultimately deliver His world, which has groaned under the cumulative burden of a long subjection.

Second, let us underscore the humanizing tendencies of Wesley's ethics. If understanding, choice, and freedom characterize humanity, and if the prevenient grace of God quickens and restores those powers in any degree, grace then is supportive of humanity or human qualities. We should celebrate the raising of humankind through grace to a position in earth's order wherein God's image is perceived anew. Supported by prevenient grace, even the one who remains a rebel is capable of lofty achievements in art or music, or other creative gifts that display the marvelous order of a world that God called into being. Wesley's ethics does not allow any diminution of emphasis on man's tragic wanderings, demonic loyalties, or heartbreak; he never ceases to magnify grace.

Third, Wesley's ethics contains great promise for an age of relativism in the structures of law. Natural law or moral is characteristic of Wesley's universe of God, angels, man, and the creatures. The sinfulness of the devil, the fallen angels, and man, have not driven God, order, purpose, or law from the cosmos. Justice, mercy, truth, and love are defined by Wesley by reference to God, not by transient societies whose ethical values may be forged by the collective will, the centers of power, or the various aristocracies of the media, the academy, the state, the worker, or the capitalist. The eternal God stands astride every human effort and every action is measured by His character and will. Wesley's ethics is characterized by freedom and responsibility within a universe governed by the God whose will is our greatest joy.

Fourth, Wesley's ethics is an ethics of promise. His eschatology is filled with dynamic hope. God's new age is to dawn in His time and it is to be the *New Creation*. His is a Wesleyan "realized eschatology," with continued fulfillment when the present world is known no more. Paradise will be restored, the ancient story given a new fulfillment, "for all the earth shall be a more beautiful Paradise than Adam ever saw."[35] The material world will then be redeemed: the animals who are "the offspring of one common Father, the creatures of the same God of love!" and, from his long exile, man with all creation will experience the fullness of Him who fills all in all.

AN EXCURSUS ON CONSCIENCE

Wesley's understanding of conscience is grounded primarily in the doctrine of prevenient grace. His comments on John 1:9 concerning Christ the Light "who lighteth every man that cometh into the world," do indeed proceed from his theology of creation. He states:

> *Who lighteth every man* — By what is vulgarly termed natural conscience, pointing out at least the general lines of good and evil. And this light, if man did not hinder, would shine more and more to the perfect day.[1]

Even here conscience is given a christological referent, but it is Christ the Lord of creation, to use Paul's designation, not the Lord of redemption.

When Wesley assesses the role and significance of conscience in the Gentile world, the world that does not have the written law, he declares that there is a law written on the heart. When the Gentiles "do by nature the things contained in the law" (Rom. 2:14), they are acting "by preventing grace." Here conscience bears witness in either accusation or defense. Wesley writes of conscience, "There is none of all its faculties which the soul has less in its power than this."[2]

What is the source of conscience? Is it something of the image of God in every person? Is it God's provision through grace to fallen humanity? The picture is somewhat mixed. Commenting on Titus 1:15, Wesley describes conscience as one of "the leading powers of the soul," which has been polluted.[3] In his sermon "On Conscience," Wesley teaches that conscience is the consequence of God's grace.[4] Yet he elsewhere appeals to liberty of conscience as a divine mandate of creation. Liberty is construed as a law of nature, which the Creator has given to every person.[5] Nevertheless Wesley's consistent position on the ground of conscience is christological and soteriological.

His approach to the question of conscience was shaped by his own Puritan heritage with its diaries and manuals and by his own sensitive self-examination, especially prior to Aldersgate. His "anguished conscience"[6] drove him to take valiant steps in order to calm its insistent voice. Only at Aldersgate, when he was "made free from the law of sin and death," was the burden ameliorated. This struggle and the subsequent respite of Aldersgate may have turned Wesley from a natural law interpretation of conscience, the common view of his century.

Analysis of Wesley's sources and reading on the doctrine of conscience shows a wide acquaintance with contemporary interpreters of the faculty of conscience.[7] This conscience literature is a distinctive genre of writings, particularly within Puritanism. Richard Baxter, Edward Young, Thomas à Kempis, Jeremy Taylor, William Law, Richard Allestree, August Herman Francke, Samuel Annesley, and Lorenzo Scupoli shaped Wesley's conception of conscience primarily in christological terms.[8] However, Wesley was acquainted with the works of others, notably Jean-Jacques Rousseau's *Emile*, Joseph Butler's *Analogy*, and perhaps his sermons, and Francis Hutcheson's *Essay on the Passions*.[9]

While the devotional writings on conscience recognized a divine source, much of the contemporary comment on morals was naturalistic. Rousseau wrote that the principles of conduct are found "in the depths of my heart traced by nature in characters which nothing can efface . . . ; what I feel to be wrong is wrong; . . . he who obeys his conscience is following nature and he need not fear he will go astray."[10]

Joseph Butler's influence on Wesley's thought is difficult to pinpoint, although we have the sharp conflict between Butler, bishop of Bristol, and Wesley over Wesley's preaching in Bristol. Butler's writings, especially his sermons, may have influenced Wesley,[11] but he was more naturalistic than Wesley could appreciate. Butler describes conscience as "the superior principle of reflection . . . in every man, . . . which passes judgment upon himself. . . . It is by this faculty, *natural to man*, that he is a moral agent".[12]

Wesley's views on conscience are hammered out most systematically in his literary debate with Francis Hutcheson. Having read Hutcheson's *Essay on the Passions* as early as 1772,[13] and prior to that the *Essay on Shaftesbury's Characteristics*,[14] Wesley responded with his sermon, which came down squarely on the side of his Puritan forebears, notably his grandfather Samuel Annesley. Hutcheson's work should be analyzed and compared with Wesley's sharp criticisms. The evidence shows that Wesley partly misread Hutcheson. Wesley sought to establish the doctrine of prevenient grace as the divine source of conscience. Hutcheson struck a naturalistic chord to him and he sought to undercut the Scotsman's logic.

In his *Essay on the Passions*, Hutcheson argued that everyone possesses a variety of senses or means of perceiving pleasure or pain. First, the external senses are the five natural powers universally recognized. A second class is called the internal sense, which involves pleasant perceptions arising from harmonious objects. A third class of perceptions is the public sense, " 'Our Determination to be pleased with the Happiness of others, and to be uneasy at their Misery.' This is found in some degree in all men, and was sometimes called . . . *Sensus Communis* by some of the Antients [sic]."[15] A fourth class is the moral sense by which "we perceive Virtue or Vice, in ourselves, or others."[16] Finally, the fifth class is called a sense of honor that causes the approval of others to be the occasion of pleasure and their disapproval to be the occasion of shame.

Hutcheson gave special thought to the moral sense as the avenue of perceiving virtue and vice. While spelling out his concepts of vice and virtue more adequately in his *Inquiry Concerning Moral Good and Evil* (1725),[17] he repeats in the essay his notion that virtue is found in that which evokes pleasure or agreeableness, and vice in displeasure or disagreeableness. Actions are virtuous because they please irrespective of advantage. The moral sense approves the virtuous and disapproves the vicious on the basis of the pleasure or displeasure evoked. But, it is argued, may not the moral sense approve the vicious and disapprove virtue? Hutcheson admitted that this may be an exceptional condition contrary to the "general Sense of Mankind," and that reason often corrects the "Report of our Senses," but indicated that any instances of such confusion or "disorder" of the moral sense would be hard to find.[18] Clearly, Hutcheson possessed great optimism regarding man.[19]

Hutcheson also discussed the relationship of virtue and God's will. He cited some who insisted that for an action to be virtuous, it must have been previously known to be acceptable to the Deity and performed with a design to please or obey Him. Hutcheson took a different view.

When a Person . . . not thinking at present of the **DEITY,** or of a *Community*, or *System*, does a beneficent Action from *particular Love*, he evidences *Goodness of Temper.* The bare *Absence* of the Idea of a **DEITY,** or of *Affections* to him, can evidence no evil. . . .

It seems probable, that however we must look upon that Temper as exceedingly *imperfect* . . . in which *Gratitude toward the universal Benefactor . . . . Perfection and Goodness,* are not the *strongest* and most *prevalent* Affections; yet *particular Actions* may be . . . virtuous, where there is no actual *Intention* of pleasing the **DEITY,** influencing the Agent.[20]

Wesley responded to Hutcheson's ideas in his own sermon on conscience. He included the public and moral sense in the idea of conscience.[21] Acknowledging that Hutcheson was correct in asserting that man is uneasy when he has done a cruel deed and pleased with a generous action, Wesley would not allow that the "moral sense" or conscience was natural to humanity. Rather, he insisted that conscience in fallen man was the gift of God, or preventing grace. As Wesley interpreted Hutcheson, the philosopher had excluded God from religion, giving Him no place in the idea of virtue; thus Hutcheson's system was atheistic. Wesley further believed Hutcheson taught that if one performed a virtuous action with an eye toward God, who either commanded it or promised to reward it, his action was without virtue.[22]

Careful analysis of Hutcheson's *Essay on the Passions* does not provide corroboration of Wesley's claims. Hutcheson was not atheistic. He did not exclude God from his scheme of virtue but argued for the virtue of actions even if they are not intentionally done to please God. Hutcheson surely perceived the superiority of actions done to please God over those done from lesser motives.[23] Yet, he argued that the beneficent action performed without specific reference to God is still virtuous. Wesley did correctly interpret Hutcheson's view concerning man, perceiving his optimistic anthropology to be in contradiction to the scriptural and historical picture of man.

What were Wesley's more systematic views on the exercise of conscience? Acknowledging his view of its theonomous ground, how does conscience function? What moves it? Is it only response to the negative, the experience of God's wrath?[24] Wesley proposed this negative position in discussing the threefold use of the law. The first use is the conviction of sin. The law "being set home on the conscience, generally breaks the rocks in pieces," and slays the sinner. Second, it is used to bring this slain sinner to Christ that he may live, and, third, to keep the sinner alive. Thus Wesley expresses himself in his sermon," The Original, Nature, Property and Use of the Law."[25]

If conscience recognizes wrong, it also has the capacity for understanding right. Conscience as the gift of God's prevenient grace must be seen as a gracious benefit, which ever impels toward the right (even when the conscience is confused in its conception or right as in 1 Cor. 8, 10). Conscience is cognizant of right and wrong according to divine norms. This does not mean that right and wrong never have social or psychological bases. Rather it means that the norms are prescribed by God, not man. Probably this is Wesley's position in the sermon "On Conscience":

It seems, indeed, that there can be no conscience which has not a regard to God. If you say, "Yes, there certainly may be a consciousness of having done right or wrong, without any reference to him"; I answer this I cannot grant: I doubt whether the words right and wrong, according to the Christian system, do not imply in the very idea of them, agreement and disagreement to the will and word of God.[26]

As a graced faculty, conscience makes moral judgments. It is an interpreter of God's mind and word to us. Its offices are to witness, judge, and execute. As witness, it testifies concerning our thoughts and actions; as a judge, it passes sentence on the morality of our acts; as executioner, it either nourishes a feeling of satisfaction (pleasure, happiness) for good deeds or uneasiness for evil actions.

The motions of conscience involve feeling.[27] Drawing upon the common fund of philosophical opinion in his century, Wesley accented the feelings of pleasure or pain that follow the approval or disapproval of conscience. John Locke, in his *Essay on Human Understanding*, had taught that the emotions were products of reason acting upon the impressions received through the natural senses. Rejecting the concept of innate senses, Locke argued that a child could be instructed that he/she could become a reasonable person. Thus, reasonable actions would be rewarded by pleasant feelings and unreasonable by feelings more or less painful. Pleasant or unpleasant feelings were based upon the experience field of each person. A person taught by a tyrant would take pleasure in unreasonable experiences. Clearly, Locke is presenting psychological experience as the basis, more or less, of moral perception. That which is good produces feelings of good and that which is bad produces feelings of bad. Locke presupposed the reasonable person whose power of reason is a mirror of the divine reason. Obviously he did not accept the doctrine of original sin in his human equation.[28]

In a similar vein, Francis Hutcheson, as noted before, had described the "public sense" and the "moral sense," which are avenues of pleasure or pain. If our neighbor is in misery, we are pained, while pleasure follows his deliverance.[29] Wesley approved of Hutcheson's position as far as it went. However, Wesley argued that these feelings of happiness or unhappiness were grounded not in human sense impressions, but in prevenient grace. Thus morality is based on a theological rather than a psychological foundation.

The feeling of pleasure or happiness is obviously the end toward which conscience thrusts us.[30] The criterion for the good or evil of an act is in the conscience, which reflects the mind and will of the divine giver. Conscience derives its moral sense from God, not nature.

In addition, conscience possesses a rational character. Wesley spoke of it as "a kind of silent reasoning of the mind," or a consciousness of the moral quality of thoughts and actions. This rational faculty may be educated, either positively or negatively. Conscience implies knowledge, or, as Wesley defined the Greek word *syneidesissis*, "the knowledge of two or more things good and evil together." The sense of sight is for Wesley an analogy for the consciousness, or recognition, of good and bad. Conscience is the faculty for knowing ourselves; it implies a knowledge of the divinely-given criteria, or norm, for guiding our lives, that is, the Word of God; and a knowledge of conformity or nonconformity to that rule.

Wesley's conclusion is clear. Conscience is a source of knowledge. Wesley's views clash with the empiricism of Locke and Hume. Although Wesley was very much the disciple of Locke, agreeing that knowledge is gained through the senses, he went beyond Locke. The natural senses cannot discern spiritual reality. Conscience, the Word of God, and what Wesley calls "spiritual senses," or "a new class of senses," are the sources of spiritual knowledge.

Here Wesley virtually describes a "super-conscience."[31] It is important to recognize that his "new class of senses" represents a distinct epistemological stage beyond conscience. In terms of the Wesleyan *ordo salutis*, the person with "spiritual sight" is either a Christian or in the pilgrimage toward faith.

Wesley recognized that conscience requires the complementary resources of the Scripture and enlightened reason ("spiritual sight") in discovering practical answers to cases of conscience. Concerning enlightened reason he declared:

> And till you have these internal senses, till the eyes of your understanding are opened, you can have no apprehension of divine things, no idea of them at all. Nor, consequently, till then, can you either judge truly, or reason justly concerning them seeing your reason has no ground whereon to stand.[32]

Elsewhere Wesley insists, "Many cases of conscience are not to be solved without the utmost exercise of our reason."[33] In his comment about ability to "reason justly," he suggests that reason must be undergirded by divine insight. Is he suggesting that a good conscience is possible only to the man or woman of faith, whose reason is divinely enlightened, who has the "spiritual sense"? Is conscience, God's graced gift, inadequate for understanding the issues of right and wrong? The answer is in the affirmative. Wesley agrees that the conscience may set forth "the general lines of good and evil" (his comment on John 1:9), but that adequate moral direction must be drawn from the Word of God and spiritual insight.

In harmony with the traditional Christian interpretation, based particularly on 1 Corinthians 8 and 10, Wesley recognizes that conscience errs. It is not infallible. The weak conscience is one "not rightly informed."[34] Conscience may also be scrupulous and this is "a sore evil." There are "some who fear where no fear is; who are continually condemning themselves without cause; imagining some things to be sinful, which the Scripture nowhere condemns; and supposing other things to be their duty which Scripture nowhere enjoins."[35]

What may the person do whose conscience thus errs? Wesley advises resistance through prayer and the help of an experienced counselor. In effect, he is suggesting the education of conscience. As Charles Gore, bishop of Oxford (1911–19) is cited: "Man's first duty is not to follow his conscience, but to enlighten his conscience."[36] Nevertheless, Wesley insists that we must assume responsibility before God for our decisions, whether based on mistaken judgments or not.[37]

CONSCIENCE: THE PUBLIC AND SOCIAL SENSE

In conclusion, Wesley's appropriation of Hutcheson's "public" and "social sense" within his (Wesley's) more realistic anthropology, provides a useful structure for Wesley's familiar commitment to liberty of conscience and social transformation. While any doctrine of Wesley's "social conscience" flows primarily from his doctrine of Christian perfection as faith that works through love, the notions of a public sense and a moral sense (both discussed in "On Conscience") do offer complementary moral categories by which he interpreted ethical concerns.[38] Furthermore, they offer the interpreter of Wesley some added clues to his theological and ethical reflection.

5

AN ETHICS OF IMITATION
The Sermon on the Mount as Paradigm

In this chapter another significant source of moral direction is analyzed. Recurrent in Christian ethical thought, the conception of Christ as moral exemplar is important to Wesley's teaching concerning the guides to ethical action. The question to be asked is: What may we see in Jesus Christ as our example for following the Christian lifestyle? From the influence of Thomas à Kempis's, *The Imitation of Christ*, through the liberalism of the Latitudinarian theologians, to the mystical theology of William Law, Wesley derived an understanding of the power of Jesus Christ as the pattern for Christian living. That a distorted understanding of imitation was corrected at Aldersgate is evident. Nevertheless, Wesley's dedication to following Christ's example and teaching continued throughout his life.

A series of thirteen sermons on the Sermon on the Mount contains the most compact summary of Wesleyan ethics. Excepting one or two pre-Aldersgate sermons, they were written by Wesley in the years from 1739–47. Considered by Mr. Wesley to provide an important basis of authentic Methodist doctrine, these sermons provide primary insights on Wesley's christological ethics. Cannon identifies Wesley's system as an ethics of realization in contrast to Luther's ethics of aspiration.[1] In the thirteen sermons the ethical motif is christological, with emphasis on learning and imitation, and sociological, with transformation of society as its goal.

Wesley's ethics stresses both outward discipline and inward perfection. He preserves his moral credo from Pharisaism by insisting that it is rooted in a new motivation. Christian discipleship entails a life of duty.

Wesley does not hesitate to list the expectations that a member of a Methodist society should accept. To *become* a member, one need only desire to flee from the wrath to come. *Remaining* in the society entailed very different burdens. In the "General Rules" for the United Societies, Wesley spoke of the history of the Methodist societies. In the latter part of 1739, eight or ten persons came to him in London, appealing to him for counsel on the way to "flee from the wrath to come." They evidenced a deep conviction of sin and were "earnestly groaning for redemption." The consequence of their inquiry was the establishment of a society in London and subsequently societies in other locations. Wesley's definition of these societies gives evidence that he was not seeking to establish a church. "Such a society is no other than 'a company of men having the form and seeking the power of godliness, united in order to pray together, to receive the word of exhortation, . . . that they may help each other to work out their salvation."[2]

The content of the "Rules" may be categorized as follows: First, those matters relating to law; second, those matters relating to gospel; and third, those matters that concern Christian piety. Wesley describes the rules in mandatory terms: "It is expected of all who continue in these societies that they should continue to evidence their desire of salvation." These are the evidences:

> There is only one condition previously required in those who desire admission into these societies,—a desire 'to flee from the wrath to come, to be saved from their sins.' But, wherever this is really fixed in the soul, it will be shown by its fruits. It is therefore expected of all who continue therein, that they should continue to evidence their desire of salvation.
>
> First by doing no harm, by avoiding evil in every kind; especially that which is most generally practised: Such is, the taking the name of God in vain; the profaning the day of the Lord, either by doing ordinary work thereon, or by buying or selling; drunkenness, buying or selling spirituous liquors, or drinking them, unless in cases of extreme necessity; fighting, quarreling, brawling; brother going to law with brother; returning evil for evil, or railing for railing; the using many words in buying or selling; the buying or selling uncustomed goods; the giving or taking things on usury, that is, unlawful interest; uncharitable or unprofitable conversation, particu-

larly speaking evil of Magistrates or of Ministers; doing to others as we would not they should do unto us; doing what we know is not for the glory of God, as the "putting on of gold or costly apparel;" the taking such diversions as cannot be used in the name of the Lord Jesus; the singing those songs, or reading those books, which do not tend to the knowledge or love of God; softness, and needless self-indulgence; laying up treasures upon earth; borrowing without a probability of paying; or taking up goods without a probability of paying for them.

It is expected of all who continue in these societies, that they should continue to evidence their desire of salvation. Secondly, by doing good, by being, in every kind, merciful after their power; as they have opportunity, doing good of every possible sort, and as far as is possible, to all men;—to their bodies, of the ability which God giveth, by giving food to the hungry, by clothing the naked, by visiting or helping them that are sick, or in prison;—to their souls, by instructing, reproving, or exhorting all they have any intercourse with; trampling under foot that enthusiastic doctrine of devils, that "we are not to do good unless our heart be free to it:" By doing good especially to them that are of the household of faith, or groaning so to be; employing them preferably to others, buying one of another; helping each other in business; and so much the more, because the world will love its own, and them only: By all possible diligence and frugality, that the gospel be not blamed: By running with patience the race that is set before them, "denying themselves, and taking up their cross daily;" submitting to bear the reproach of Christ, to be as the filth and offscouring of the world; and looking that men should "say all manner of evil of them falsely for the Lord's sake."

It is expected of all who desire to continue in these societies, that they should continue to evidence their desire of salvation,

Thirdly, by attending upon all the ordinances of God. Such are, the public worship of God; the ministry of the word, either read or expounded; the supper of the Lord; family and private prayer; searching the Scriptures; and fasting, or abstinence.

These are the General Rules of our societies; all which we are taught of God to observe, even in his written word, the only rule, and the sufficient rule, both of our faith and practice. And all these, we know, his Spirit writes on every truly awakened heart. If there be any among us who observe them not, who habitually break any of them, let it be made known unto them who watch over that soul as they that must give an account. We will admonish him of the error of his ways; we will bear with him for a season: But then if he repent not, he hath no more place among us. We have delivered our own souls.[3]

The ethics of imitation is the oldest ethical dimension in Wesleyan thought. Based on Christ's teaching and example of holiness of life, the believer is called to the imitation of Christ. The Christian is to be like Christ, marked by the perfection of the Father (Matt. 5:48).[4] Acceptance of Christ as our pattern means following the way to the goal. Imitation ethics therefore is theological. Far from being the complete saint, the follower is being shaped by the daily process of obedient faith.

To understand the centrality of Christ, the pattern in Wesley's ethics, we should note the obvious influence of Thomas à Kempis's *The Imitation of Christ*. A decisive force in Wesley's "conversion" in 1725, this fifteenth-century treatise from the Brethren of the Common Life taught that "simplicity of intention and purity of affection" must characterize our lives. Thomas à Kempis wrote that the Christian is to make "his [Christ's] Holy Life the Object of our Imitation, and to form our Dispositions and Actions upon the perfect Model of that bright Example."[5]

Wesley's sermons on the Sermon have been described by Sugden as "a practical manual of Christian conduct."[6] According to Wesley, the Sermon is divided into three branches. In Matthew 5 is found the "sum of all true religion." Matthew 6 gives rules for that "right intention which we are to preserve in all our outward actions." Matthew 7 deals with hindrances to religion.

In the Beatitudes, Wesley sees stages of the Christian journey to heaven. Although we lack conclusive evidence, it is probable that the Eastern church's vision of the Christian life as successive stages toward a goal influenced Wesley's interpretation.

Poverty of spirit is described as the foundation of Christian life. It defines those to whom God has "given that first repentance, which is previous to faith in Christ." Whoever knows this has been made deeply aware of the "loathsome leprosy of sin," the constant bias to think of himself "more highly than he ought to think." The "kingdom of heaven" is understood by Wesley in soteriological terms—salvation from sin. Man as sinner is unable to follow Jesus' example, but the

Savior's death means the death of sin and the opening of the way.

Mourning succeeds the poverty of spirit. Wesley addresses the experience of the "absent God," when the believer feels the sorrow of heart in the time of trial or the oppressions of inward sin. Meekness describes a composure of mind, not of those who "resent nothing, because they feel nothing," but balance preserving the mean, avoiding extremes. Wesley uses Matthew 5:21–26, concerning anger with one's brother, as an illustration of meekness restraining anger. The meek inherit the earth in receiving God's daily gifts but also in sharing in the glory of the new earth.

Righteousness is the image of God, which He gives to those in whom this "strongest of all our spiritual appetites" is awakened.

Mercy is received by those who themselves display it. Wesley equates mercy with the love of neighbor, amplifying its meaning by discussing 1 Corinthians 13. Sermon two concludes by an impassioned argument against warfare between Christian kingdoms, and against intolerant Christian churches who convert sinners by burning them alive. "It is your Father's good pleasure yet to renew the face of the earth. Surely all these things shall come to an end, and the inhabitants of the earth shall learn righteousness."[7]

Purity of heart means to be cleansed from "every unholy affection." Wesley, having briefly defined purity, illustrates the beatitude by reference to the sexual purity discussed by Jesus in Matthew 5:27–32. It is evident that Wesley recognized other forms of impurity beside sexual impurity; pride and anger are specifically mentioned.

Purity of heart or inward holiness is to manifest itself in outward life. The pure are peacemakers who hate strife and contention, and who seek to mediate hostility. Defining his terms broadly, Wesley describes doing good to all as the mark of the peacemaker. To do good to friend or enemy, to assist the poor, the sick, and the hungry, is his lifelong work. Wesley concludes that the pure and the peacemaker shall be persecuted, but that in these qualities are found "the fundamentals of Christianity," the quintessence of religion. Most importantly he writes, "Behold Christianity in its native form, as delivered by its great Author! This is the genuine religion of Jesus Christ! Such He presents it to him whose eyes are opened. See a picture of God so far as He is *imitable by man*!"[8]

The imitation of Christ means much more than inner piety. The Sermon on the Mount immediately moves from piety to practice, emphasizing that the Christian is the salt of the earth and the light of the world. Wesley develops from this passage his most powerful exposition of the social character of Christianity. The particular religious problem he addresses is the mystic doctrine of "stillness," found both in William Law and in the Moravian brethren. The sermon was preached on February 3, 1747 and is one of Wesley's greatest ethical statements.

Wesley criticizes those who would drive Christian faith inward, working "all virtues in the will," and withdrawing from the world. This has been called "the grand engine of hell." Christianity is essentially a social religion and to turn it into solitary piety means its destruction. True faith grows in a community of persons. Certainly solitude is required, but it must be succeeded by a return to society. The virtues of mercy and peacemaking occur only among persons. Indeed, Wesley argues, intercourse with the ungodly is necessary to the development of meekness, patience, mercifulness, and other holy tempers.

> This is the great reason why the providence of God has so mingled you together with other men, that whatever grace you have received of God may through you be communicated to others; that every holy temper and word and work of yours may have an influence on them also. By this means a check will, in some measure, be given to the corruption which is in the world.[9]

The sermon echoes the themes of imitation both in personal life and social transformation. Wesley emphasizes the latter by showing that heart religion will shoot forth branches of outward obedience. This means for Wesley the exercise of "works of mercy," avoiding unnecessary expense in food, furniture, clothes, the waste of time, or the practice of needless employments. The entire purpose of such stewardship is that we may "enlarge our ability to do good."[10]

Discourse five on the Sermon wrestles with the relation of law and gospel. Jesus did abolish the ritual law of Moses, but not the moral law. This law was given for all persons in all ages, resting on the nature of God and man, and the unchangeable relation between God and man. The command to love is law; as promise it is gospel. The law leads to gospel; the gospel enables a more exacting fulfillment of law.

Wesley's ethics incorporates a central concern for moral standards. Wesley neither presumes that keeping the law will be simple nor that it is impossible. Sinful man lacks the inclination to keep the law, and therefore, lacks the power. The motivational force is evil, not good. These are they who break the Lord's commandments (Matt. 5:17–20). However, there are those who "do and teach" the Lord's commands. It *is* possible to follow Jesus' commands by the *power of love*. Love is not a simple human possibility, but it is possible by divine grace. Wesley reiterates a lifelong theological position, that justification is by faith and that faith works by love.

The righteousness that God gives exceeds all that may be attained by those who strive to keep the law. Indeed, self-acquired righteousness is nothing. The rigorous efforts of the Pharisees are praised by Wesley, but he recognizes that human attempts at fulfilling the moral law are vain because they lack goodness and purity.

Wesley proceeds to show the significance of intention in our pursuit of God. Rooted particularly in what he had learned from Thomas à Kempis and Jeremy Taylor, "purity of intention" expresses the Wesleyan solution to the deep gulf between aspiration and attainment in ethics. Jesus teaches that our actions may be acceptable to God "by a pure and holy intention." Prayer or alms giving are not forbidden by our Lord, but if performed that they may be seen by men, they are wrong.

Intentionalism is important in the entire moral life. In jurisprudence, the issue of intent is continually raised. Wesley recognized that purity of intention was crucial to the life lived according to God's will. Gustafson has applied a philosophical distinction to motives and intentions, defining the former as "backward-looking reasons" for action and the latter as "forward-looking reasons" for action.[11] What Gustafson calls motive might be Wesley's "intention."

To continue analysis of Wesley's preaching from the Sermon, we should note that the Lord's Prayer is described as a pattern, model, or standard for our prayers.[12] In prayer, alms, or fasting, and in our ordinary lives we are to be regulated by purity of intention. Wesley cites William Law's *Serious Call* to show that the Christian may not separate secular from sacred tasks. Wesley freely paraphrases Law, substituting the words "pure intention" for Law's "heart truly devoted to God."[13]

The "single eye" of Jesus' teaching (Matt. 6:19–23) becomes for Wesley the figure for purity of intention, the eye fixed on one thing. When the eye is single the search for earthly treasure will not consume the soul.[14] Wesley usually treats wealth and riches as highly dangerous. However, riches may be used for God's glory and for the needs of family and the poor. The intention makes the difference. The imitation of God begins and continues in the spirit of our minds. " 'God is a spirit;' and they that imitate or resemble Him must do it 'in spirit and in truth.' "[15] The service of mammon is the imitation of the world. It is impossible to be transformed by the renewal of the mind while one is conformed to the present world. Wesley asked, "Do you obey God? Are you zealous to do His will on earth as the angels do in heaven?. . . . then you set the world at open defiance. You trample its customs and maxims under foot, and will neither follow nor be led by them.[16]

In summary, Wesley's ethics incorporate important emphasis upon imitation and renunciation. James Gustafson has detailed the moral significance of Christ as pattern.[17] This is a recurrent theme in Christian ethics from the Sermon on the Mount to the medieval mystics and Abelard, from the pietists to Wesley, from Ritschl and Charles Sheldon[18] to religious liberalism and the Anabaptists. Christ as the pattern to follow in discipleship is a theme that knows no narrow identification with a particular theological school. However, the theological anthropology of particular systems sharply influences the responses of an imitation ethics. Wesley takes his stand with those who believe that discipleship is possible when God acts in grace, forgiving sin and bringing new life. Christ's example is presented as a challenge to those who follow. Imitation of His pattern is indeed the "impossible possibility," as Reinhold Niebuhr expressed it. Wesley never overlooks the great difference between man and Christ; but he never permits human sin to become the dominant note. Grace strikes the chord of promise and hope that resounds above all the dissonance of sin. Man may do the will of the Father in the power of His Son and Holy Spirit.

A POSTSCRIPT ON INTENTION

Wesley's desire to retain the possibility of pure intention despite flawed execution leads to some problems. One issue is the tendency in Wesleyan thought to treat poor execution more lightly than required, provided of course that the intention is good. Wesley managed this problem better than his heirs, maintaining a Lutheran conviction of the need for continued penitence because of the "involuntary transgressions" that the best of persons commit. The subtle sin of pride (or ignorance) has kept some persons from acknowledging that an action may be sinful when the intention behind the act is good. Not to recognize the flaws in the way we carry out our purposes is to live in blindness. Intention, when overvalued to the neglect of the consequences of our decisions, is responsible for great moral loss. Unintended false accusation is still damaging to a person's reputation. Intentionalism must be balanced against the consequences that flow from it, even if the consequences lack any grounding in the logic of the intention. In other words, injury may be totally foreign to the particular intention, but should it occur in an action based on the intent, the actor must bear responsibility. Wesley probably did not clearly articulate this problem; the result is that the feeling of culpability is diminished in the experience of some of his spiritual heirs. The moral consequence of an act is deemed to be less significant than the morality of intention. Perhaps this may explain why some have tended to internalize faith with a weakened concern for external issues.[19]

Gustafson has drawn attention to the abuses of intention in Catholic casuistry. The exercise of mental reservation, probabilism, and similar styles of thought were mercilessly satirized by Blaise Pascal in the *Provincial Letters*. Using a refined form of mental gymnastics, wrong behavior could be justified by the intention of the actor. Many Protestant writers avoid the concept as too susceptible to manipulation. Gustafson writes of intention, "It can become a defensive device of moral self-justification, and a rationalistic device that assumes a deed is determined in its moral aspects of intention alone."[20] This essentially is my argument above. Nevertheless, to minimize the concept of intention is to propose a deed-centered ethics, which does not evaluate why a certain action is performed. The problem is not resolved by appealing to God's purposes and intentions, which form man's. In Christian theology, our intentions are formed in response to God's purposes, whether in trust or in revolt. Failure to stress intent as a central human responsibility is to move toward cancellation of human moral agency. Jesus gave intent central importance in the moral life when He argued that the sin of adultery could take place in the eye, or mind, alone, whether or not a physical consummation took place. If intention is "settled belief about future actions,"[21] then the mind's intent is morally equivalent to the act itself. The intentions must be formed in accordance with the teachings and example of Jesus Christ.

6

CHRISTIAN LOVE
The Key to Wesley's Ethics

The imitation of Christ means to commit ourselves to the commandment of Jesus that we love God fully and our neighbor as ourselves. An ethics of love involves a commitment to pure intention, and to deeds of love that express the intention with integrity. Love is central to Wesley's ethical structure. In the essay that follows we will seek to comprehend the meaning of love, especially in its relationship to trusting, saving faith.

When Charles Wesley wrote his "Love divine all loves excelling, joy of Heaven, to earth come down . . .," he expressed what was at once the great work of Wesleyan hymnody and the essence of the theology that John Wesley articulated through a long life of love toward God and man.

The historical factors that converged upon Epworth and Oxford, shaping John Wesley into the consummate witness of the Christian theme of love, have yet to be adequately traced. How did it happen that of all the thinkers in nearly two millennia of Christian history who pondered the meaning of love, Wesley should achieve such a maximum view of the concept? Who else has surpassed Wesley in his perception of holiness as love, socially active, catholic in temper, personally integrative, unitive, liberating?

Other Christian thinkers, including Augustine, Bernard, and the mystics wrote warmly and compellingly of love. Augustine powerfully contrasted two loves that challenge our lives: "Two cities have been formed by two loves: the earthly by the love of self, even to the contempt of God; the heavenly by the love of God, even to the contempt of self."[1] The Christian mystic often spoke in rapturous transport of the glories of Christian love, until the spirit seemed to be a sounding board of the harmony and unity of God. "Jesus the very thought of thee, with sweetness fills the breast . . . But what to those who find? Ah, this, nor tongue, nor pen can show: the love of Jesus, what it is, none but his loved ones know" (Bernard of Clairvaux).

Nevertheless, there often were deeply ingrained flaws in the vision that Augustine, Bernard, Richard of St. Victor, Thomas à Kempis experienced. Augustine's concept of love was distorted by his theological pilgrimage through the noble paganism of Plato and its revival in neo-Platonism as well as the more exotic system of the Manicheans, both of which denigrated the material creation in their zeal to emphasize the realm of the spirit. The effect of this bifurcation of matter and spirit entailed a misunderstanding of the biblical idea of love, which balances the forms and expressions of love in a pattern of wholeness. Augustinians were never able to crush Eros but were continuously striving to insulate the world of spirit against the powerful winds of flesh. Much the same must be said of the mystics and to a lesser extent the pietists, and of many Christians. Wesley did not escape it either even though he had little affection for the theology of "St. Austin," as he called him. The romances of Wesley show us both a spirit of warm, tender love, and a reticence that was exaggerated by a deep concern over the possible conflict between human love and Christian duty.

As a mature man he wrote:

> Many years ago I might have said, but I do not now,
> > Give me a woman made of stone
> > A widow of Pygmalion.

> And just such a Christian one of the Fathers, Clemens Alexandrinus, describes; but I do not admire that description now as I did formerly. I now see a Stoic and a Christian are different characters.[2]

Recognizing as we should the limitations that characterized Wesley, we must not allow ourselves and those to whom we preach to miss the centrality of the doctrine of love in Wesley. Olin Curtis, a sympathetic, knowledgeable exponent of Wesley has opined that he "had almost the same epochal relation to the doctrinal emphasis upon holiness that Luther had to the doctrinal emphasis upon justification by faith, or that Athanasius had to the doctrinal emphasis upon the Deity of our Lord."[3] Always to be remembered is Wesley's normative understanding of holiness, both inward and outward, as love.

LOVE OF GOD AND NEIGHBOR

Love is the central Christian virtue elaborated by Wesleyan ethics. It is a composite principle that incorporates the personal and social dimensions. It is rigorously demanding and radically challenging, for in Wesley, love and perfection are linked together to form a lofty ideal. This is love perfected, an ethical challenge that influences the whole range of Christian thought and action. The perfection of love that Wesley so often stressed was consistently the same love that Jesus taught:

> Thou shalt love the Lord thy God with all thy heart, and with all thy soul, and with all thy mind. This is the first and great commandment. And the second is like unto it, Thou shalt love thy neighbour as thyself. On these two commandments hang all the law and the prophets (Matt. 22:37–40 KJV).

The idea of perfection stressed by Jesus is summed up by the concept of wholeness. The whole heart, mind, and soul committed to God in a loving relationship, and the same intensity of love and quality of love that is bound up in self-love is to be expressed toward the neighbor. There are loves of various kinds in human experience that are not necessarily Christian. "What makes it Christian," writes Knudson, "is its permeation with the Christian ideal of moral perfection."[4] Differently expressed, love is Christian when it participates in the nature of God, who Himself is love, and reaches outward from oneself to others. It is love rooted in the divine nature and turned toward God's creation. Because God is perfect and God is love, Christians, according to the New Testament are to participate both in the perfection and love of God. We are called to act in the sphere in which we live as God does in His Kingdom that we may be the children of our Father in heaven (Matt. 5:45). Our relationship to God is determinative of our behavior. "Be ye therefore perfect, even as your Father which is in heaven is perfect" (Matt. 5:48 KJV). The two commandments to love are indivisible.

What then does Christian love have to do with ethics? It is the new life of love that permeates our affections, will, and intellect, shaping relationships with others, influencing decisions, and forging thought patterns that are in conformity to the mind of Jesus Christ. Love sets the tone for action, helps set Christian priorities, and inspires to the realization of the Christian's calling. In Christ all things become new.

Love, as Wesleyan theology and ethics articulates it, is frequently interpreted as intensely individualistic. This represents a deficiency of understanding. Love, according to the New Testament, is a word of community, of social significance. It is precisely so with Wesley: "The Gospel of Christ knows of no religion, but social; . . . *Faith working by love* is the length and breadth and depth and height of Christian perfection" (emphasis mine).[5] In addition to this argument, Wesley holds a concept of the church as *koinonia* and community. For him, *koinonia* means "holding things in common,"[6] and this is descriptive of the style of the church, especially the primitive church. Wesley frequently speaks of the church as a society or community.[7] So prominent is this note in Wesleyan ecclesiology that Gordon Rupp has argued that with Wesley a fourth mark of the church has been added to other Protestant views of the church. Along with the other marks or notes—the Word faithfully preached, the sacraments rightly administered, discipline exercised—stands the mark of community. With Wesley the importance of the church as community is now recognized, especially the idea of the "Christian cell."[8]

The primary implication of this Wesleyan focus on love, community, and *koinonia* is that the Christian must seriously engage in what Bonhoeffer has called a "worldly Christianity." Wesley would say that holiness, perfect love, is "at home" in the world. It flourishes in abrasive contacts with Christian and non-Christian persons. The solitary Christian is an anomaly; "holy solitaries," like the "holy adulterer," represent a perversion of Christian faith. Separation from the world in order to further the life of holiness involves a contradiction of the gospel. Holiness happens in the world. The life of mercifulness or peacemaking can only be realized among saints and others. It is Satan's perversion of God's purpose, the "grand engine of hell," that deceives people into believing that God's will is realized by withdrawal.[9]

Albert Knudsen, a contemporary Methodist, perceptively argues the case for the social character of love in his discussion of the principle of love:

The Christian ethic is an ethic of love, and it is such because the Christian world is a personal world and a personal world is a social world. If the Christian world were a mere collection of individuals, each with his private aim and destiny, the fundamental ethical principle of Christianity would be purity or perfection. . . . But the Christian world is not such a world. . . . The real world is a world of mutually dependent beings. It is a social world of interacting moral beings; and in such a world love is necessarily the basic moral law.

Knudsen further asserts that love and perfection include each other. "Perfect love is moral perfection and moral perfection is a state of perfect love."[10]

FAITH THAT WORKS THROUGH LOVE

A second major biblical principle in Wesley's ethics, more doctrinal than the *summa* of Jesus, is the Pauline assertion in Galatians 5:6 that the gospel is not bound up in rites of Judaic legalism but is incarnated in the faith that works by love. John Wesley's translation in his *Explanatory Notes Upon the New Testament*, and his consistent translation, is "faith which worketh by love," although he once writes: "Faith working or animated by love is all that God now requires of man."[11] Of crucial importance in the Pauline dictum is the word translated "working." Does the word emphasize faith more strongly than love? The answer seems to contain important implications for ethics. *Energoumenē* is a participle, present tense, middle voice. Machen indicates that the middle voice conveys the idea of the "subject acting on something which is part of itself." Dana and Mantey agree stating that it describes the "subject participating in the results of the action."[12] What this suggests is that we may not interpret Galatians 5:6 in a way that weakens the integral relationship of faith and love in Christian life. Wesley's own note reads, "Faith-alone; even that *faith which worketh by love*— All inward and outward holiness."[13]

Lightfoot wrote concerning verse 6 that these words "bridge the gulf which seems to separate the language of St. Paul and St. James. Both assert a principle of practical energy, as opposed to a barren, inactive theory."[14]

The value of this study of the text becomes apparent if we compare the ethics of Wesley with the ethics of Luther. Lutheran ethics has been given careful attention in Paul

Althaus's *The Ethics of Martin Luther*. He makes a clear case for the primacy of faith in Luther's ethics. As Althaus puts it, "Luther's ethics is determined in its entirety, in its starting point and all its main features, by the heart and center of his theology, namely, by the justification of the sinner through the grace that is shown in Jesus Christ. . . ." Justification is seen "as the presupposition of all Christian activity," and "the source of all Christian activity."[15]

In ourselves we are sinful before God, but by God's gracious gift we become righteous. The justified one has a twofold character; *simul justus et peccator*, at one and the same time justified and sinner. In the experience of God's justifying love we are enabled to love our neighbor. In other words, faith results in action or good works. Christian activity flows out of the experience of God's love, and this activity is itself love, sharing all of the characteristics of the love of God who justifies.

While Lutheran ethics stresses the primary force of faith and justification, resulting in love, or Christian activity, Wesley's ethics is rooted in love, or holiness. Primary to Wesley's social commitment is love. As Wesley was previously quoted: "The Gospel of Christ knows of no religion, but social; no holiness, but social holiness. Faith working by love is the height of Christian perfection."[16] Faith is described by Wesley as the clear source of justification, and like Luther he stresses that good works are the "immediate fruit" of faith. Luther insists, in his *Preface to the Epistle of St. Paul to the Romans*, that faith is "a living, busy, active mighty thing. . . . It is impossible for it not to be doing good works incessantly. It does not ask whether good works are to be done, but before the question is asked, it has already done them, and is constantly doing them."[17] Wesley is concerned to stress the greater significance of love. Faith in Christ is to be preached so as to produce holiness or love. He insisted, "Faith itself, even Christian faith, the faith of God's elect, the faith of the operation of God, still is only the handmaid of love. . . . Yea, all the glory of faith . . . arises hence, that it ministers to love; it is the great temporary means which God has ordained to promote that eternal end."[18]

Love is promoted by faith and involves grateful love to God, which leads to love for our neighbor.

Comparing Luther and Wesley we may argue that, despite the great similarity of many of their views, Luther's is primarily an ethics of justification while Wesley's is an ethics of sanctification. Luther's is an activism of faith while Wesley's is an activism of love. All Christian activity grows out of the life of holiness or love. Luther stresses faith active in love as clearly as does Wesley, but his focus is on justification, which leads to works of love, whereas Wesley's concern is faith active in love, which means for him the clear and actual creation of love in the heart as the result of faith. The law of love is now written on the heart, a new consciousness is given, life is brought under a new law of love, a *real* change happens in the life, resulting in a life of love toward God and neighbor.

James Gustafson wrestles with the difference between an ethics of justification and an ethics of sanctification. He suggests that for Luther, Christ alone is true sanctification. Through the Holy Spirit the Christian can grow in faith. In faith, the Spirit works through our person (Luther uses the figure of a water fountain or water pipe to describe love coming from God and flowing to neighbor in our acts of love). But while there is a view of sanctification in Luther, it is less significant than justification. Gustafson has written:

> Texts that Wesley . . . used to preach on the possibility of a transformation of will, consciousness, and love receive at the hands of . . . Luther . . . a more dialectical treatment. One can say that for the former . . . the benefits of Christ's righteousness become man's righteousness, though man is always dependent upon God's grace, For Luther, . . . though man participates in Christ's righteousness, it does not become something man virtually possesses.[19]

This seems to be the case with Galatians 5:6. Quite obviously both Wesley and Luther stress both justification and sanctification *but* place special stress upon sanctification or justification respectively. Luther tends to stress freedom to love, a freedom that faith in God gives. He is free to love the neighbor, to be Christ to the neighbor. Nevertheless there is always the twofold character; man is sinner and justified. Man is forgiven, but not healed of sin. Righteousness is not something we possess. It is God's, not ours, existing as *objective* to the self. Love too is God's, not ours. Whenever Christians love the neighbor, it is Christ loving through us. The Christian possesses the power to love, but the power is objective to the self. And the capacity to love is limited by the continuance of the sinfulness of the Christian man. The moral life is thus diminished in its power.

For Wesley, love is the fruit or consequence of faith, but

love, or sanctification, is magnified above faith. Faith is the means to holiness. "Faith . . . is the grand means of restoring that holy love wherein man was originally created. It follows, that although faith is of no value in itself, . . . yet as it leads to that end, the establishing anew the law of love in our hearts, . . . it is on that account an unspeakable blessing to man."[20]

Of course, Wesley cannot separate faith from love and holiness. Wesley indicated that "holiness (salvation continued) is faith working by love."[21] For Wesley the life of love, or holiness, is a life of good works. Holiness, love, and good works are inseparable. The door to these is faith. Faith opens the heart to love and active works. The life of holiness is a life of progress in works of love, which nourish and perfect in faith. Now living under the "law of faith," the Christian is required only to experience the faith that is animated by love. Commenting on James 3:22, Wesley asserts that

> faith has one energy and operation; works, another; and the energy and operation of faith are before works, and *together with* them. Works do not give life to faith, but faith begets works, and then is perfected by them.
>   Faith hath not its being from works (for it is before them), but its perfection.[22]

Wesley seems to argue that love and good works are virtually the same, or at least inseparable. A life without good works is not a life of love; therefore, it is not a holy life.

I suggest that Wesley stresses the relationship between holiness, love, and good works so insistently because good works are the outflow of the holiness, or love, received in Christ. Apart from this outreaching love, holiness has no content. The holiest saints need the merits of Christ without interruption. God does not "give them a stock of holiness. But unless they receive a supply every moment, nothing but unholiness would remain."[23] If holiness is best defined as love, failure to love (or do good works) means lack of holiness. It means that the personal participation in Christ is circumvented by failure to love. "For our perfection is not like that of a tree, which flourishes by the sap derived from its own root, but . . . like that of a branch which, united to the vine, bears fruit."[24]

In summary, Wesley stresses an organic, natural union, or relation with the Spirit. Good works flow or grow from that relation. The basic motivations or intentions are made whole or are characterized by health. The recurrent tendency to pride is overcome so that good works do not threaten to become works of righteousness as long as the organic relation is sustained. Good works grow within the holy life and are integral to that life. Luther emphasized an instrumental concept wherein the Christian is a more passive conveyor of the life of the Spirit. Good works are the works of Christ flowing through the believer, while the believer himself is *simul justus et peccator*. Thus, there is a significant difference in Wesley and Luther.

IMPLICATIONS

In this comparison between Lutheran and Wesleyan theology, what issues are at stake that bear on the question of ethics?

First, it is evident that certain serious aberrations across the Christian centuries seem recurrent in each of these systems of theology. The ethics of faith alone, or justification, has borne the potential for quietism, moral indifference, antinomianism, complacency, lack of passion for holiness. Justified, experiencing the pardoning love of God (but yet a sinner), one stands in the grace that frees. "In Christ, man is given freedom from concern about saving himself; he is freed from earning moral and religious merits."[25] The *sola fide* position does not ask as its *primary* question: "How can I live the Christian life?" but rather, "What must I do to be saved?" The answer is that faith is required, and not works. Despite all that Luther could say about the fruit of faith, the central concern remained justification not sanctification or good works. Christian activity is good despite our sinfulness, because it is done in faith.

Why is it that the ethics of justification seems limited in moral challenge, even when, as in Luther, there are precise teachings that call for good works? For example, Luther will declare that the believer has the Holy Spirit, "and where he is, he does not permit a man to be idle but drives him to . . . the practice of love toward all men,"[26] or, in other words, to sanctification. No simple answer is available, but one may suggest that the ethics of justification with its *simul-justus-et-peccator* dialectic, and the freedom it bears, makes moral passivity *possible*. If the justified person is a channel through which love, or the Spirit, flows, this may result in ethical "stillness" as it did for some of the *Unitas Fratrum* of Zinzendorf. As Daniel Benham expressed it in 1856 in his *Memoirs of James Hutton*, Wesley's great commitment in contrast to that of Zinzendorf was to the doctrine of "an *active love*, proceeding from the new birth and faith; and manifesting itself in *striving* after *holiness* and *Christian perfection*, and to the doctrine of the furtherance of this *active* love by the *means of grace in the church*. Zinzendorf on the other hand allowed of none other than a *grateful love*, proceeding from the . . . heart of a *pardoned* sinner.[27]

While we are contrasting Luther and Wesley, this comparison of Wesley and Zinzendorf seems to give a clue to the differences between Luther and Wesley. Luther was no quietist, but the effect of his intensive preaching of faith alone seems to have lacked the moral stimulus toward the life of spiritual maturity or holiness, with its implication of good works, that he so zealously proclaimed in his *Freedom of the Christian Man* and elsewhere.

Another kind of problem is recurrent in the ethics of sanctification, the danger of complacency again, buttressed by a mistaken sense of completeness, the feeling of "having arrived." (This contrasts with the opposite kind of complacency that remains content with little because "arrival" is firmly disavowed in this finite life.) There is another peril of the loss of the freedom gained through faith in an excessive spiritual psychologizing; a "pulse taking" that easily becomes self-oriented and transfers the vision from "Christ in me," living in me and working out through me, to the quality and character of *my* actions, thoughts, and words. The implication of this, especially for Christian social ethics, is that the Christian's call to love the neighbor as one's self is forgotten in one's intensive assessment of the force of his love or the quality of his prayer life. *Social ethics becomes a threat to personal ethics.* Faith is no longer active in love.

Wesley preserved his ethics from that sort of excessive preoccupation with personal holiness by his insistence on the life of Christian growth. He insisted that holiness is salvation continued, faith working by love.[28] In his teaching and practice, he made clear that Christian perfection, or sanctification, "implies a continued course of good works" that is inseparable from those good works that follow faith.[29]

The ethics of love, or sanctification, does not incorporate a view of man as passive, but as actively striving to live out the life of love to God and neighbor. The ethics of holiness is an ethic of the Cross, a cruciform ethics wherein the divine and human intersect and unite. It is an ethics of the Cross in that it means that the Christian voluntarily takes up the Cross, seeking to share more and more in the life of God. Sanctification ethics thus *seems* to lack something of the freedom or spontaneity of the justification ethics, by its deliberate quest for holiness. Ever risking works righteousness it avoids antinomianism and Pelagianism by its continued insistence on a need for Christ's righteousness, which then is worked out by love toward others.

Such a rigorous ethics escapes the perils of a faith ethics while *risking* pride and self-fulfillment, and ever presses the believer toward a religion of love. If this sometimes seems to result in a more austere ethics, it may be argued that the Cross suggests a course of life that entails stress. He who follows the ethics of love takes up his cross voluntarily as the way to the realization of Christ's will. Luther, on the other hand, emphasizing the freedom of justification (our standing before God as justified, freed, saved) did not consider one's cross a burden to be willingly picked up, but emphasized the "pressing cross" of Christ: the Cross pressed upon us, as it was pressed on Simon on the road to Calvary.

The ethics of Wesley places a greater claim upon the Christian person. The Wesleyan doctrine of Christian perfection does not ostensibly admit of the recurrent presence of sin in the life of the sanctified Christian.[30] Many of Wesley's interpreters have overlooked or even rejected Wesley's secondary definition of sin, thus giving credence to the charge that they espoused "sinless perfection." In his *Plain Account of Christian Perfection,* a 1767 compilation of his essential teachings on the subject, Wesley makes clear his position that the Christian continually requires the merit of Christ's death. Why is this so? Here Wesley offers a second concept of sin, which is only a "hair's breadth" from Calvinism. The Christian needs Christ continually because sin occurs in every person outside of and without the consent of the will. Wesley described this as "involuntary transgression." Every human being is a person, an ethical being, responsible for the actions that follow choices, whether those choices seem to be moral or not. Persons are contingent, dependent. Their lives continually interact with the Creator and creation. Whether the will is involved or not, a person is always response-able. When the person becomes conscious of a prior action with wrong motivations or harmful consequences, the will responds either by acknowledging the "involuntary transgression" to be sin or else excusing the action and therefore seeking to cover it (i.e., the sin of Adam). But suppose the person never becomes conscious of the wrong? Still, it is "sin."

Why is "involuntary transgression" sin? As all of Wesley's interpreters know, Wesley preferred to define "sin" as being characterized by consciousness and volition. If an action is "known" to be wrong, and the will gives "consent" to that act, sin is practiced. The moral seriousness of that kind of decision seemed to Wesley to be far greater than the transgression that flows from man's finitude. (This definition is in fact little different than the legal distinction between murder, wherein there is conscious decision, and manslaughter, which lacks such prior motivation.)

If Wesley sought to preserve this kind of juridical distinction, he did not relieve the person committing an "involuntary transgression" from the moral consequences of that "sin." Chosen or not, the particular act is still transgression of God's perfect law. Since Wesley believed with Anselm that the sacrifice of Christ was necessary to atone for the violation of that law, he argues that the violator must be forgiven and covered by the death of Christ. Nothing man offers is meritorious. Continuous trust in the sacrifice of the Cross is necessary, for man has stored up no treasury of merit to offer for sin.

There is a wide divergence between an ethics of justification with its concomitant of imputed righteousness (where the Christian's whole life is one of subjective sinfulness along with objective justification, and where the Christian's whole life is one of repentance (Thesis 1 of Luther's 95 Theses), and an ethics of holiness where righteousness is decisively bestowed *in the living personal relationship* with Christ. The latter ethics emphasizes purity of intention, while admitting deficiency in the execution of intention. The life of love does not insure a perfect personal relationship, or form the basis for a perfect social ethics. It does insist upon a kind of rigor and discipline that the faith ethics does not imply. In Tillich's words the ethics of justification asserts: "Simply accept the fact that you are accepted."[31] The ethics of holiness incorporates a tension that makes that kind of Reformation theology difficult to accept, even though one of the consequences of the passion for holiness is at times a nervous kind of Christianity that strips the Christian life of joy and power. I do not argue that the ethics of holiness *necessarily* bears this sort of "worried mind"; but historically, among both Catholics and Protestants, this intensity has borne heavily upon many who have sought to practice the presence of God by the disciplines of the holy life. It is quite clear that this was the burden of Wesley's theological pilgrimage until after Aldersgate, as he struggled for sanctification before he understood the reality of faith and justification. With his understanding of the Pauline principle of "faith active in love," Wesley seems to have brought into balance the life of faith/freedom/justification and that of love/discipline/sanctification. Albert Outler writes that "the life of faith is a life of discipline, nurture, effort," or in a word, sanctification.[32] The doctrine of Christian love, faith that works through love, is thus the central principle in Wesley's Christian ethic. [33] Faith is never demeaned. It is the means to love, which perfects faith. Nevertheless, love is the key in Wesley's theology to *personal* and *social* ethics. The life of love, good works, and holiness involves both the personal and social. In Wesley's sermon, "The Scripture Way of Salvation," the personal and social dimensions of holiness, or love, are articulated in a discussion of two kinds of good works, both necessary to sanctification. First are "works of piety," including prayers, receiving the Lord's Supper, reading the Scripture, fasting—all rather specifically personal and interior. Second are the "works of mercy," the ministering to the souls and bodies of men and women in prison, sick, lonely, and naked, alienated from God.[34] These two kinds of works seem to reflect the Wesleyan way of *balancing personal and social concerns.*

CONCLUSION

It is time for many who have listened long to the cliches about Wesleyan individualism to see that Wesley had a deep sense of social compassion and concern. It is not hit or miss, growing out of Wesley's warm heart but is the result of careful biblical exegesis and preaching. It is also time to remember that Wesley did plow deeply into the soil of his society, attacking slavery before Wilberforce was born, supporting civil and religious liberty against a threatening radicalism, warning the nation about economic practices that ignored the weak and poor, developing perhaps the first clinic in London, preparing practical studies on medicine and electricity for healing the sick, and setting up spinning and knitting shops for the poor. By his own testimony he had spent twenty-six or twenty-seven years during his leisure hours studying anatomy and physics, although he had only "properly" studied them during the months of the voyage to Georgia in 1735. As the revival moved forward in power, Wesley saw the human wreckage that his age so tragically scattered about it. He began anew to study medicine, sought the advice of an apothecary and a surgeon, and began to invite those in his societies to come to him who were sick, some ruined by medical expense. Serious illnesses he left to physicians who were chosen by the patients.[35]

What was the motivating principle behind this ceaseless activity? To save souls and lead people into holiness? Wesley would say that this is asking the wrong question. His concern was wholeness: physical, psychological, spiritual, intellectual. The principle that shaped the man and his movement was faith working through love.

In 1759 and 1747, respectively, Wesley wrote two works: *The Desideratum: Or, Electricity Made Plain and Useful. By a lover of Mankind, and of Common Sense* and *Primitive Physick: Or, An Easy and Natural Method of Curing Most Diseases.* [36] At the conclusion of the *Primitive Physick*, Wesley wrote, "And this I have done on that principle whereby I desire to be governed in all my actions: Whatsoever ye would that men should do unto you, the same do unto them."[37]

Elsewhere he indicated his motivation for these works to be faith working through love. The Christian's love is universal, generous, disinterested, "his love resembles that of Him whose mercy is over all His works. It soars above all these scanty bounds, embracing neighbors and strangers, friends and enemies—yea, not only the good and gentle, but also the forward, the evil, and unthankful. . . . By experience he knows that social love, the love of our neighbor, is absolutely different from self-love, even of the most allowable kind."[38] Thus, in conclusion, this claim is made: Christian love, or holiness, is the key not only to Wesleyan personal ethics, but undergirds his social ethics.

7

AN ETHICS OF THE SPIRIT

An ethics of Christian love rests upon the life of the Holy Spirit, for love is the Spirit's fruit in the Christian believer, not one of the instrumental gifts of the Spirit. Love is teleological. It is the very purpose and goal of God's Spirit to form unselfish love in His church. Given the Spirit as the overflowing river of God, the church's mission is to carry out spiritual, moral, and social transformation.

In this chapter we seek to give structure and substance to Wesley's theology of the Holy Spirit and its ethical significance for social change.

TASK AND PURPOSE

It was Jesus who, having lived out most of His brief life of ministry, prayed concerning His infant community: "I do not pray that thou shouldst take them out of the world, but that thou shouldst keep them from the evil one. They are not of the world, even as I am not of the world. Sanctify them in the truth; thy word is truth. As thou didst send me into the world, so I have sent them into the world" (John 17:15–18, RSV). The force of these words seems clear enough. Christians belong in the world as Jesus belonged; Christians are models before the world, not copies of it—Jesus was that kind of example; Christians possess a moral dynamic, a perfectness that fits them to live in the world,[1] not away from it as cloistered saints, like an aseptic lab culture (growing in artificial conditions) in a stoppered test tube. Jesus was a perfect man, a whole person, sent into this world to make it whole. Christians are sent to live where they may represent Jesus in their lives of spiritual power.

When Jesus in this context prays for the sanctification of His followers, He is repeating essentially what He said in the Sermon on the Mount, "Ye are salt," "Ye are light." Sanctification makes men and women inclusive, not reclusive. It means a life lived for many, not for one. To make the claim is not to deny that it is personal; to assert that it is personal is to admit that it is social. Nothing personal is ever truly private because it in some way will leap from one person to another.

If the church, then, is to be a moral force in the world, it will become this as it is energized and driven by the Spirit. By "driven" I mean what Søren Kierkegaard described in his parable of the rich man who bought a team of excellent horses for his own pleasure and the pleasure of driving them. After a year or two, these fine horses had become dull and drowsy, thin, and weak. Finally, he called in the king's coachman and asked for help. After one month the spirit and carriage of the horses was so changed that no horses could be found in the land to match them. Why? The owner was not a coachman, but merely played coachman. The horses were driven according to the horses' conception of how they should be driven. This is a picture of human life. Man was given vast powers, but he used them according to man's conception of the way they should be used.

> Once it was otherwise. There was a time when it pleased the Deity Himself, if I may say so, to be the coachman, and He drove the horses according to a coachman's conception of what driving is. What was man not capable of then! . . .
>
> No man has ever lifted his head so proudly in elevation over the world as did the first Christians in humility before God. As that team of horses could run on thirty miles without stopping to pant, so did they also run—ran seventy years in a stretch without getting out of the harness; without pausing any place. . . . They said, "It is not for us to lie down or loiter along the way. We make our first stop—in eternity!" It was Christianity which was to be carried through, and they carried it through, indeed they did! But they were also well-driven, indeed they were![2]

The church—a driven fellowship! How does the church live within that spiritual presence so that it may be the leaven that leavens the whole lump, salt to preserve the earth, light to illumine, energize, and heal? The answer will be found, I believe, in the biblical teaching concerning the Holy Spirit, in what may be called an ethics of the Spirit.

This chapter is an attempt to spell out an ethics of the Spirit based on Wesley's theology of the Spirit. It is conceived as an exercise in constructive theological ethics, parallel to James Gustafson's *Christ and the Moral Life*. Its purpose is the creation and elucidation of a Christian social ethics grounded in the biblical theology of the Spirit. We must avoid a monism of the Spirit or an ethics which is not truly Trinitarian. Much attention, however, has been given to the ethics of God the Creator (an ontological ethics, or an ethics of creation), and the ethics of Christ the Redeemer (a christological ethics, an *imitatio* ethics, etc.). An ethics of the Spirit has been neglected as surely as has the entire theology of the Spirit. This essay proposes to correct this imbalance by wrestling with the ethical significance of the life of the Spirit in the experience of the Christian community and beyond that in human community. However, balance is always uncertain in these boundary issues. Wesley teaches that the present work of the Spirit in the world is convicting, assuring, sanctifying, illuminating, and contributing toward a positive, transforming ethics.

HISTORY OF THE ETHICS OF THE SPIRIT

An ethics grounded in pneumatology has been discredited historically. The struggle of the church to define and explicate a Trinitarian theology has of course shaped the church's ethics of the Spirit. The tendency in much Christian thought is toward subordination of the Spirit to the Son and the Father. The issue is unresolved. The Eastern Orthodox Church still raises the ancient question whether the Holy Spirit "proceeds" from Father *and* Son,[3] a crucial question in the famous East-West schism, which began as early as the Third Council of Toledo (589) and culminated with the divided church in 1054. Wesley is satisfied to affirm the equality of Spirit, Son, and Father.[4]

A theology of the second person often seems dominant, even as it is in the Apostle's Creed, or in the theology of Barth according to some of his interpreters. Wherever that is the case, a christological ethics becomes ascendant with focus upon such emphases as suffering, imitation, substitution, and the incarnational. The ethics of many Anabaptists is decidedly christological. The soteriology of Anselm or Luther's doctrine of justification by faith alone is christological, placing special attention upon the objective work of Christ and the imputation of his merit to man. This kind of attention leads to an ethics that is more objective than subjective. An ethics of God the Creator contains its own particular *foci*, such as the natural law approach to ethics in Catholic moral theology, and in Wesley's moral critiques of slavery and his affirmation of human rights.

What is clearly required is a Trinitarian ethics, a complementary ethics, which maintains the integrity of the relationships within the Trinity. Such an ethics will be ontological (rooted in the doctrine of God the Creator), christological (Redeemer), and pneumatological (Spirit), or, in other words, faithful to the biblical exposition of the work of the Father, Son, and Holy Spirit. This structure is offered in Wesley's theology of creation, particularly in the concept of *imago Dei*; in his theology of salvation, or new creation, which deals with reconciliation and faith that works through love, and in the theology of the Spirit with emphasis on purity of intention and empowerment for ministry. In delineating an ethics of the Holy Spirit, we run the risk of a unitarianism of the Spirit, but the clear intention is to develop an ethics of the Spirit, which we may integrate with ontological and christological ethics. If that is accomplished, we may then begin to develop an ethics that is holistic. Even as Father, Son, and Holy Ghost are ever One, so Christian ethics in the Wesleyan mode will be integrative, unitive, holistic. We must preserve both unity and diversity ("procession" may be a better word) in the metaphysics and ethics of Christian revelation.

It seems evident enough in Christian ethics that there is a limited interest in the Holy Spirit. The books on ethics give little coverage to the Spirit's work despite the biblical accents on the Spirit's moral influence (See Gal. 5). Some persons, either aware of historical aberrations or prudently concerned over exaggerations in spiritual phenomena, are leery about this area of biblical teaching. Dr. Luther's antipathies for the *Schwärmer* (enthusiasts) reached a crescendo when he reputedly criticized Müntzer for acting as if he had swallowed the Holy Ghost, feathers and all. This fear of excess or extremes is not without basis as the tragedy of Münster attests.

Perhaps the chief theological peril is a "unitarianism of the third person."[5] An interesting expression of this may be seen in the charismatics who remove the cross from the chancel or steeple and replace it with a dove (which raises the issue of theological symbolism). It is one thing to develop a Trinitarian theology, which integrates a theology of the Spirit, and quite another to work with a theology of the third person, which seems to make Him contemporary with the church while the work of the Father and Son belongs to days past and gone. A theology of the Spirit is always Trinitarian; Father, Son, and Spirit are ever interpenetrative, and no work of God is ever compartmentalized. To be rooted in the testimony of the ancient faith, found in the Scriptures, one must always do justice to both the monotheism and Trinitarianism of the New Testament.

A Trinitarian ethics is an ethics of the Spirit. It expresses the creative concern of God; His intention to go out from the circle of His infinite completeness, or perfection, to the circumference of a living human community; the restorative concern of Christ to renew humanity and bring it into the fullness of His life. Such an ethics is predicated upon the Spirit's concern to universalize and actualize this outgoing intention of God and this reaching forth of Christ Jesus. The Spirit proceeds (or goes forth) from Father and Son.[6] Thus, it is the divine economy to be in community with man, making the human spirit self-transcending, like God's Spirit.

DEFINING AN ETHICS OF THE SPIRIT

By an ethics of the Spirit, we specifically intend the *scientific* (meaning here the science of ethics) *analysis* of the manifestation of the Spirit in the sphere of moral life. We are describing the ethical dimension of the Spirit's influence. For example, when I suggest that the ethics of the Spirit is creative, I do not mean to attribute creativity to the ethical system. Rather, I submit that any analysis of the Spirit's ethical influence will recognize the creative dimension of the Spirit's work.

This ethics is grounded in the life of the Holy Spirit. It takes into consideration the realm of spirit, both Holy Spirit and human spirit. It asks: How does the Holy Spirit influence the human spirit in the ethical dimension?

ESSENTIAL ASPECTS

We define the ethics of the Spirit as Christian, evangelical, social, and spiritual.

Christian

It is a Christian ethics. This means that the ethical content of the Holy Spirit's work and ministry is ever christocentric. As the Western church has maintained, the Holy Spirit proceeds from the Father and the Son, that is, He is the personal "going forth" of God and Christ to humanity. Jesus said concerning the Spirit: "He shall glorify me, for he shall receive of mine, and shall show it unto you" (John 16:14). Wesley wrote that the Spirit is the One "uniting our hearts to Christ."[7]

Evangelical

Wesley's ethics was consistently evangelical. The possibility of living a Christian moral life is grounded in the proclamation, hearing, and reception, by faith, of the gospel. Recognizing as he did that prevenient grace makes it possible for everyone to make moral distinctions and thus to apply in some manner theocentric criteria to social issues, Wesley always sought the transformation wrought by the gospel as the most adequate basis for effecting change. For it is in the power of the gospel, present in and expressed through the ecclesiastical community, that the task of social change is carried on in its most healthy forms. Apart from the evangelical dimension, the task soon becomes old, the reformers cynical, the energies jaded. The life of the Holy Spirit is at the heart of personal and social righteousness.[8]

This evangelical motif is amplified in a broader Christian context by Hendrikus Berkhof, who claims that St. Luke's teaching of the fullness of the Spirit does not receive its full emphasis until we recognize its "external consequences."

> People began to prophesy, to exclaim, to praise God, to be Christ's witnesses, to speak in tongues, to . . . speak the word of God with boldness. . . .
> The filling by the Spirit means that the justified and sanctified are now turned, so to speak, inside out. In Acts they are turned primarily to the world; in Paul primarily to the total body of Christ; but this is merely a difference in situation and emphasis.[9]

We further propose an evangelical ethics as integral to an ethics of the Spirit. Jesus taught, "When the Spirit of truth comes, he will guide you into all the truth." "And when he comes, he will convince the world concerning sin and righteousness and judgment." Further, He declared, "But when the Counselor comes, whom I shall send to you from the Father . . . he will bear witness to me; and you also are witnesses" (John 16:13, 8; 15:26 RSV). The ethics of the Spirit is infused with the mandate for witness to the good news that "God was in Christ reconciling the world unto himself" (2 Cor. 6:19). Concurrently we proclaim the good news that life in the Spirit means a life of moral power.

Social

The work of the Spirit is a social work. His movement in the church and in the world is analogous to the communion of the Trinity. His work in church and world is toward unity and community. The Holy Spirit creates in the church a community of faith and hope and love. Wesley amplified the social character of the church in presenting as a company of those "called by the gospel, grafted into Christ by baptism, animated by love, united by all kinds of fellowship." His description of the church as a community of love, giving of their goods for the needy (Acts 2:44–45), is consistent with his entire understanding of the church as a community of faith and love. The community of goods was "a natural fruit of that love wherewith each member of the community loved every other as his own soul."[10]

Christians are called to live out their Christian testimonies in human society, comprised of good and evil persons. Christianity is a social religion. It cannot survive in isolation. It is God's work to change the lives of men and women, "yet he generally doeth it by man."[11] The community of the Spirit is the society by which the Spirit brings transformation. The procession of the Spirit is ever social. Within the Trinity there is a procession of the Spirit from the Father, through the Son. The Spirit is the outreach of God toward the world, drawing those who believe into the circle of God.

Spiritual

Self-transcendence is the essence of spirituality, the capacity of spirit for going beyond the self, participating in the other, taking the other into itself.

We recognize the self-transcending character of the Holy

Spirit. This is true even of the human spirit, even though the consistent tendency of man to be *incurvatum in se* (curved inward) is recognized. "Spirit" possesses the possibility of going beyond self.

The name and concept called "spirit" is frequently employed but often misunderstood. Wesley defined spirit as an expression of the image of God, suggesting that the volitional, ethical, and rational are aspects of the spiritual dimension of man.[12] A distinguishing mark of humanity is its capacity for self-analysis and reflection. We think! We reflect on our actions and shape our subsequent actions. Our response isn't mere response to stimuli, but rather involves a self-extrapolation in order that we may look back at ourselves. More surely, when the Spirit of God lives in us, when we walk in the Spirit, an ecstatic potential is realized.

John Macquarrie suggests that *spirit* "names a kind of being that is somehow shared by man with the Spirit of God. Spirit is present in and constitutive of man as well as God." This, however, does not define spirit. Macquarrie continues:

> Spirit may be described as a capacity for going out of oneself;
> . . . Man is not closed or shut up in his being. . . . To him
> there belong essentially freedom and creativity, whereby he
> is able to shape (within limits) both himself and his world. It
> is this openness, freedom, creativity, . . . that makes possi-
> ble . . . the formation of community, the outreach of love
> and whatever else belongs to . . . the 'life of the Spirit.'[13]

OPERATIONAL ASPECTS

To proceed farther, the ethics of the Spirit developed through Wesley's theology will consider the creative, sanctifying, liberating, dynamic, and permeative dimensions of the Spirit's work. In the earlier set of categories (Christian, evangelical, social, spiritual), the emphasis seems to be on *essence* or *nature* of an ethics of the Spirit. In this second set of descriptions, we are dealing with the *operational* aspects. We analyze the Spirit's *action*, the *ethos* of the Spirit.[14] A social ethics grounded in the theology of the Spirit will emphasize the following five areas.

The Creative Work of the Spirit

The creativity of the Spirit is of crucial significance in an ethics of the Spirit. The Spirit's work possesses a structured, formative character; it includes both form and content. An ethics of the Spirit must retain this, while emphasizing that "the wind blows where it wills." There is both form and content, structure and ecstasy in the Spirit's work. The Spirit of God, we are informed in the creation story (Gen. 1), moved upon the formless deep.

The ethics of the Spirit will emphasize the creativity of the Holy Spirit and the human spirit, the freedom of the spirit and its responsibility, and the openness and development of the moral life of man. Ethics will interpret that developing moral life to the church and the world. This, it may be suggested, is what St. Paul is emphasizing in his charge, "Walk in the Spirit" and in the challenge to reproduce and develop the fruit of the Spirit. In its social outworking, the life of the Christian community will be formative, creative, and unifying. It is the task of Christian ethics to explicate how this will be actualized.

In Wesley's interpretation of the creative Spirit he looks to the Genesis creation where the Spirit moves on the face of the waters. The Spirit of God is the "First Mover," Wesley writes.[15] The Spirit also moves in the new creation, making us over. This change is called being born again, "because as great a change then passes on the soul, as passes on the body when it is born into the world."[16]

Sanctifying Work

A concomitant emphasis in the ethics of the Spirit is His sanctifying work. The Spirit's operation in the moral life will be characterized by wholeness, sanctity, integration, purity of heart. In its social dimension, the sanctifying work of the Spirit will mean judgment, healing, growth in righteousness. Methodist theologian, Nels Ferre, has a persuasive discussion entitled "Distinctive Dimension of Christian Social Action" in his *Christianity and Society*. He strongly presents the concept of the sanctifying work of the Spirit in social transformation. Commenting on the essentials of Christian social action, Ferre suggests as the highest emphasis, *the explicit recognition of the direct activity of the Holy Spirit as the incomparably primary dimension of Christian social action—*and of the Spirit of God for that matter [Ferre distinguishes between Holy Spirit and Spirit of God], on the level of general social action. To keep institutions under judgment because of their sins is one important aspect of Christian social action.[17]

However, this is not the center of social action. What is the heart of Christian social action? Ferre speaks forthrightly, "It is not man's wisdom, or experience, or effort, individually or socially. It is the active presence of the Holy Spirit."[18]

It is in the Spirit that one participates in the dimension of perfection. "The distinctive dimension of Christian social action is man *in loco perfectionis* [in the place of perfection]. Though man is still imperfect through both finitude and sin, when he is open in intention and deed to the Holy Spirit, God performs through him the miracle of creative change and vital healing."[19] Ferre insists, finally, that *agape* is the greatest gift of the Spirit, since it is God sharing His own nature with man.

Wesley's contribution to the doctrine of the Holy Spirit represents some of his most significant analysis. In an age where "enthusiasm" was so fervently deplored, Wesley insisted that it was not fanaticism to believe in the immediate, present reality of the Spirit. Enthusiasm is defined as "a *false imagination* of being inspired by God; . . . one that fancies himself under the influence of the Holy Ghost, when, in fact, he is not." [20] Fanaticism, however, cannot destroy the authenticity of the Holy Spirit's presence and activity. In "A Farther Appeal to Men of Reason and Religion," Wesley appeals to the Scriptures, especially John 14 and 16, Romans 8, and 1 Corinthians 2 to support his claim that the Spirit's presence may be expected and acknowledged.

Looking backward, he cites traditions to prove the spiritual reality that the body of Christ has always perceived to present in the world. Chrysostom, Jerome, Origen, and Athanasius are cited, as is Bishop John Pearson of the Church of England in the seventeenth century. The *Book of Common Prayer*, from Archbishop Thomas Cranmer, is recalled by Wesley with its superlative collect for the Eucharist, "Cleanse the thoughts of our hearts by the inspiration of thy Holy Spirit."[21]

Fully convinced of the immediacy of the Spirit's life and presence, even in his era, Wesley pressed for the recognition of that presence in every sphere of human life, particularly in the human spirit, and in the church.[22] When John Wesley articulated his doctrine of sanctification, he was concerned with its personal and social dimensions. Concern for personal purity through the cleansing blood of the Cross was paired with concern for Christian love expressed in good works. What is the goal of sanctification according to Wesley? The answer: That the Christian might live as a Christian in the world. This means bearing the servant role, performing both works of piety (service to God) and works of mercy (service to mankind). It means the practice of holy living in the daily routine of human existence. Sanctification is love performed in every sector of the common life. All of this happens because the sanctifying Spirit is flowing through the Christian like a river of living water. Starkey sees in Wesley's teaching the positive correlation between "the Sanctifying work of the Holy Spirit and the Transformation of man and society."[23]

What elements in the Wesleyan theology of the Spirit provide undergirding for his social ethics? These may be expressed in terms of the Spirit's work: the work of regeneration, the work of cleansing, the work of assuring, and the work of empowering. In ethical terms the Spirit's work means the transformation and redirection of motivation.

The Spirit's work of cleansing is particularly pertinent to the spiritual preparation of the servants of the Lord. To live and serve in the world was recognized by Jesus to be an experience of tribulation. The consistent New Testament declaration of enmity between the kingdom of God and the kingdom of the Devil underscores the need for the Christian to live out of a resource not one's own. The life of faith is a warfare. Jesus fought this battle and won it because of the presence of the Spirit upon and within Him. Despite all of the threats of the world, Jesus knew that the history of salvation is worked out between God and His servants in living dialogue with men and women in the real world. He prayed for preservation of His disciples in the world, not their isolation or withdrawal from it.

This is Wesley's vital interest. Holiness—the fullness of the Spirit—is the qualification for life in an evil world. Michalson contrasts the worldliness that idolizes the world with the Christian worldliness, which "removes the distraction of idolatry and thus liberates a man to assume responsibility for that world. Without that liberation, one could turn the world into an idol to which he felt responsible, thus losing his capacity to be responsible for it."[24] Asked the question, "But would not one who was thus sanctified be incapable of worldly business?" Wesley responded: "He would be far more capable of it than ever, *as going through all without distraction.*"[25]

Liberating Work

Liberty is the third point of emphasis in the Spirit's activity in social change. St. Paul's Roman and Galatian letters give particular attention to this work of the Spirit. "For the law of the Spirit of life in Christ Jesus hath made me free from the law of sin and death" (Rom. 8:2). Living in the Spirit and walking in the Spirit are perceived as the essence of liberty. Liberty for Paul is always truncated and barren except when held in place by the ethical obligation of love. "For, brethren, ye have been called unto liberty; only use not liberty for an occasion to the flesh, but by love serve one another" (Gal. 5:13). One of the Wesley hymns expresses the dynamic of Christian liberty:

> Come, then, and dwell in me,
>   Spirit of power within,
> And bring the glorious liberty
>   From sorrow, fear, and sin;
> The seed of sin's disease,
>   Spirit of health, remove,
> Spirit of finish'd holiness,
>   Spirit of perfect love.[26]

The liberating dimension of the Spirit's work is bounded by ethical guidelines. This liberty is a fruitful ground wherein love, joy, and peace may develop. There is no law against love, joy, and peace. However, there is a law that enters into their growth. They will not mature where liberty has forfeited its ethical grounding.

The liberation emphasis is of crucial significance in much contemporary theology—in the Latin American, female, and black liberation movements in our time. An ethics of the Spirit will not take us from these spheres of action. It will call us out into the world where economic slaveries, human indignity and oppression, poverty and disease, hold persons under purgations more severe than most of us are able to imagine. A Christian, evangelical, social, and spiritual ethics is the answer to human cries for liberation.[27] Other answers are given that are attractive and challenging to Christian answers. However, an

Blah ? *Blah*

evangelical ethics requires *announcement* of the message of
Christ's liberating work through the Spirit to the world.

What do you mean?

Dynamic Work

The fourth concept to consider in the operational dimension is the dynamic. An ethics of the Spirit emphasizes the
Spirit's empowering work. There is a moral force that the wind
of the Spirit brings to the ethical spheres of life. Without this
force creativity and sanctity remain lifeless concepts, structure
without substance, body without breath. Bernard Ramm
affirms this imperative:

> An ethical theory without a realistic doctrine of maturation is
> but a paper theory. . . . It is an empty ethical theory which
> believes it can determine the right or good but offers no
> theory how men concretely achieve the right. . . . Part of the
> uniqueness of biblical ethics is that the doctrine of the Holy
> Spirit is at the center of its ethical system. The Holy Spirit is
> the motivator in Christian ethics. . . . Essential Christian
> morality is . . . written on the human heart—the wellspring
> of action—by the Holy Spirit. The point is that the Holy
> Spirit is in the heart of the Christian exercising his moral
> presence.[28]

In the dynamic of the Spirit may be developed the creative
and sanctifying characteristics in human community. In this
empowerment we may see believers undergirded to carry out
the world-transforming mandate that has been given to the
Christian church. "You are the salt of the earth," Jesus said.
"You are the light of the world" (Matt. 5:13–14). We must resist
the futility of hiding our lights under a bushel, or, to recall
Nietzsche, the lighting of lanterns in the morning.[29]

Wesley believed that the power to live out the promise of
the Christian ethics was given through the Holy Spirit. In itself,
humanity is helpless to overcome the degenerative force of sin.
"Without the Spirit of God we can do nothing but add sin to
sin; . . . it is He alone who worketh in us by His almighty
power, either to will or to do that which is good."[30] Wesley, in
language of superlative optimism anticipates that the "grand
'Pentecost' shall 'fully come' whereby the Church shall become
a glorious force" attended with the demonstration of the Spirit
and of power.[31]

In Wesley's theology of the Spirit, there emerges a

corollary between the Holy Spirit's empowerment and His assuring work. The witness of the Spirit is one of the distinctive aspects of Wesleyan thought. When the teaching is applied to the Spirit's work in the world, it suggests a dimension of moral presence in the Christian evangel. St. Matthew referred to the wonder of Jesus' audience as they listened to His Sermon: "The people were astonished at his doctrine: For he taught them as one having authority, and not as the scribes" (Matt. 7:28–29 KJV)

In Wesley's own experience the witness of the Spirit was revolutionary. If Aldersgate may be seen as the *locus* for this divine witness to Wesley, it demonstrates the incredible difference that spiritual assurance of adoption makes.[32] The certainty that we are in God and He in us is crucial to our ability to live and bear witness courageously. Not to know to whom we belong, to waver between the many options, is to be incapable of adequate service. The Spirit creates positive loyalty. The person who stands uncertainly before the world is incapable of world-transforming potential. The Holy Spirit removes the distractions of the divided mind by directing Christians toward one master. The witness of the Spirit, then, is not simply a private, subjective event for the pleasure of the recipient. It is the *sine qua non* for dynamic service.

Permeative Force

Finally, we must stress the permeative power of the Spirit in the church and the world. The influence of the Spirit is present throughout the earth. We may speak of this aspect in terms of common or prevenient grace. The Spirit is salt, light, water, and wind. He permeates the sphere of spirit. The Spirit blows where He will.

Here, then, are five points that spell out the action of the Spirit. They are familiar to all who deal with ethical issues. We suffer great loss when we shift these emphases on ethical action from their Christian, evangelical, social, and spiritual context.

The ethics of the Spirit will be a conversionist ethics. In both the individual and social dimensions of human experience, the Spirit of God acts to transform, to heal, to create and re-create. H. Richard Niebuhr, in wrestling with the relationships between Christ and culture, has defined the conversionist position as that which takes into account the fallenness of human nature and the fact that culture bears and transmits this perversion. The conversionist further recognizes the opposition between Christ and human institutions and customs. Yet, this does not lead to separation but to an integration. "Christ is seen as the converter of man in his culture and society, not apart from these, for there is no nature without culture and no turning of men from self and idols to God save in society."[33]

In the history of Christian ethical thought and expression, several types of response to society have become manifest. H. Richard Niebuhr has been very influential in his discussion in *Christ and Culture*. His fivefold typology is highly useful and often subtle. A less complex typology may be employed that describes the Christian response to culture as the pattern of either domination, separation, or permeation.[34] The first pattern leads to political and triumphalist interpretations of the church. The second suggests a sectarian and pacific interpretation, a theology of the Cross. The third pattern entails a theology of the Spirit, a pattern of involvement in the world and penetration of its structures with the dynamism of love.[35] The ethics of the Spirit is an ethics of faith, hope, and love, offering the most scripturally balanced, holistic framework for shaping the world. While there are surely authentic scriptural elements in each of these responses, they lack the full orb of the transformist position which is the Wesleyan commitment.

THE COMMUNITY OF THE SPIRIT

In the Acts of the Apostles the church is presented as preeminently the community of the Spirit. As the community of the Spirit, it is concerned with all things spiritual. If we can agree that the spiritual is somewhat synonymous with becoming a person in the fullest sense, and if we can hold that in a christocentric context, then we may argue that the church must participate in all spheres of action that enhance personality.

The community of the Spirit is a driven community, an ecstatic organism, a surging spirit. Driven from its sacred enclosures, its interior temples by the Holy Spirit, the spirit of the Christian man stands beside other human spirits. The spiritual community thus becomes a transforming community in the larger human society, challenging and transforming spirit. The community of the Spirit is a community of faith and love. As Paul Tillich so pointedly writes, "If the Divine Spirit breaks into the human spirit, . . . it drives the human spirit out of itself. The 'in' of the divine Spirit is an 'out' for the human spirit. The Spirit . . . is driven into a successful self-transcendence."[36]

In an ethics of the Spirit, the church transcends itself, its hesitations, its clinging to prerogatives, and becomes in the Spirit a searching wind that tries the hearts of men and the structures of world community or discord. It is central to the biblical theology of the Spirit to say that even as God who is Spirit transcends Himself (goes out from Himself) and becomes the God who is with man, the community of the Spirit also will be self-transcending, going out to human community at large. The community of the Spirit is self-transcending by its very nature as a spiritual fellowship. "Spirit" means going forth from, proceeding from, self-overcoming. This is the theological basis for a Christian social ethics.

The Christian community belongs in the community of humanity! What metaphors best symbolize the penetration of the world community by the Christian community? The church as: Island? Peninsula? Beachhead? River? Ocean with tributaries?

None of these seem sufficient. The best metaphor is wind, breath, life-giving, vivifying. Here the church is seen as the *ecclēsia tou pneumatou*, the "community of the wind." Wherever the wind blows there is change, transformation. The community of the Spirit, blowing in the wind, breathing upon the structures of the age, transforms. The life-giving Spirit in the church reproves of sin, creates right relationships, and warns of judgment to come. Whoever is not born of water and the Spirit shall not see the kingdom of God.

The community of the Spirit alone is able in the Spirit to transcend itself and to become immersed in the structures of the world, to be witnesses and martyrs, a sanctifying agency. Its forum is less the cloister or the sanctuary than the marketplace. Its redemptive work is carried out in full view of the world. He who said, "Ye are the light of the world. A city set on an hill cannot be hid," was Himself slain, not in some remote dungeon but on a hill. The public spectacle of martyrdom challenges the pretensions of the world; the Cross casts its shadow across the ways of Caesar and denies his claim to lordship. Martyrs of the church and living witnesses so penetrate the structures of the age that the dying Roman Empire summons its apologists to charge the church with its declining health. The church's rejoinder is given in Augustine's *City of God*. The empire's ill health is the result of its pride. It is striking that the church should be credited with such an infiltration. That, however, is what the church will be in the world. The living church is bent upon personal and social transformation. Even if it deliberately avoided all themes except personal salvation, its concern for the community of humanity would break out everywhere. Christianity that does not begin with the individual does not begin. Christianity that ends with the individual ends. The church spends and is spent in creating righteousness and in challenging unrighteousness, in personal and community forms.

THEOLOGICAL CONTENT OF AN ETHICS OF THE SPIRIT

Here it becomes important to raise other questions. What is the content of an ethics of the Spirit? How does the ethics shape the church's relation to the world?

The answer to the first question takes us back to our earlier suggestion that the ethics is creative and sanctifying, liberating, dynamic, permeative. This we may present as the form of the ethics. But what or who is it that is creative and sanctifying? The Holy Spirit who creates and sanctifies! The content of His creative, sanctifying work is faith, hope, and love. Faith, hope, and love are theological virtues and spiritual virtues. Each includes inherently the spiritual or self-transcending quality, i.e., the person who possesses faith, hope, and love, lives in the Spirit and goes forth from the enclosed circle of distrust of faith, from fear to hope, from self-love to divinely ordered commitment. Faith, hope, and love are spiritual graces and are clearly ethical in content.

The ethics of the Spirit is an ethics of faith. This is relational in expression. It is characterized by trust, conversion, renewal, repentance, and justification. Each of these implies change. Trust means giving oneself away in dependence on another (or, going out from oneself). Conversion is becoming a new person, a person for others. Repentance and justification are relational changes, the mind and attitude of God toward man and man toward God being transformed and brought into a unitive state.

An ethics of faith is personal and social. As applied to the social situation, it would imply that the Spirit is at work in the efforts that exist to bring change of mind among mankind. Attempts at healing the discords that rend human societies, the distrust between economic institutions and labor, the political alienations, the social gulfs, are the result when the Spirit works faith in the church and the church works out the ethics of faith in the world. The Spirit is at work in the world through the church and even without the church. The church never works dynamically apart from the Spirit.

The ethics of the Spirit is an ethics of hope. Hope is a continuously restorative power, characterized by an ultimate optimism, and balanced by a preliminary measure of both confidence and doubt about the completion of that which man sets out to do. What this means for Christian social ethics is the overcoming of the apocalyptic pessimism so prevalent in some current evangelical (is this the good news?) discussions. It is equally a corrective to the glorious but unrealistic dreams of progress espoused by some Christians in the nineteenth century, both liberal and evangelical.[37]

Lycurgus Starkey, writing concerning the Wesleyan interpretation of the Holy Spirit's work of sanctification, asserts:

> A social gospel grounded in the Holy Spirit's work of sanctification would need no buttressing by the enlightenment's illusions of inevitable progress and natural perfectibility. . . . Just as God purposes to bring individual Christians to a holiness of heart and life, so through his church God works to bring about a person-in-community holiness to the whole of society as a foretaste and indispensable part of his coming Kingdom. . . .
>
> God works for the transformation of men and society; hence we must work.[38]

Daniel Migliore of Princeton writes concerning the theology of hope:

> I think that the theology of hope can help by providing a biblically-grounded perspective for responsible Christian social and political action.
>
> It is concerned with man as a political being and not simply with the individual and his private destiny. . . . A political theology aims not simply at interpreting the world differently but works toward its transformation.

The theology of hope bears an understanding of God as the One who worked in the historical process to bring justice and peace among men. The church is the community of the hopeful, "the source of continual new impulses toward the realization of righteousness, freedom and humanity here in the light of the promised future that is to come."[39]

A spiritual ethics is, lastly, an ethics of love. *Agape* epitomizes the work of the Spirit. As St. Paul so triumphantly announces to the Corinthians: "Love bears all things, believes all things, hopes all things." Love believes, love hopes. Love is the greatest of all because it actualizes faith and embodies hope. Paul sums up the essence of walking in the Spirit by asserting the ethical challenge to love (Gal. 5:6, 13–14, 22–25).

It is this central concern that represents the genius of the Wesleyan ethics. As Mildred Wynkoop has emphasized, the social ethics of Wesley is the ethics of love that permeates the world and strives for its transformation.[40]

CONCLUSION

In his chapter, "Spirit and Spirituality," Macquarrie comments on the positive possibility of spiritual achievement (to go out from oneself) by an individual but questions whether groups are able to realize that elusive quality. Social conflicts abound, demonstrating how unspiritual the life of society is. Can this ever be changed, he asks? Will social morality always be "a matter of power politics"? Is it true that groups will rarely give up power unless they are coerced.

> But surely Christian spirituality envisages a broader strategy than the spiritualization of the individual. In calling the church "the community of the Spirit" we are implying that here there is . . . a society with the capacity to go out from itself. It has been said that the church is the only society which exists primarily for the benefit of the non-member. To be sure, the church has been often just as defensive, self-regarding and unspiritual as any other group. But whenever and wherever it is learning to be truly the church, the community of the Spirit, it is introducing a new dimension into the social situation, one that gives hope for an eventual transformation.[41]

HOPE! Is not this part of the vision that St. Paul described: "For through the Spirit, by faith, we wait for the hope of righteousness" (Gal. 5:5, RSV).

In conclusion, we may call the church to a Christian discipleship in all spheres of life. If the church, with its vision of righteousness and wholeness, rooted in a "radical monotheism,"[42] is excluded from social involvement, then whom will the church suggest for the task? The sectors of power and influence, professions and business, labor and politics, have no adequate ethical ground from which to re-create, sanctify, and energize. These sectors of power all have particularized ethical norms for self-regulation, but lack an ethic equal to the depth of human demand and need. George Forell, in answering the question: "Why did the church not speak up against Nazism? said, "Now, this church should have probably said more. But when all is said and done, the only people that said anything were the churches. Certainly the legal profession said nothing. Certainly the schools and the university professors said nothing." There was no university *Kampf*, or a medical association *Kampf*. The only *Kampf* in Germany was the Kirchenkampf, Forell asserted.[43] This illustrates my claim that the community of the Spirit is able to speak because it possesses the ethical force. The ethics of the Spirit—Christian, evangelical, social, spiritual, and creative, sanctifying, liberating, dynamic, and permeative—offers both the structure and substance (form and content) of a "categorical imperative" to humankind. The ethics of the Spirit offers the content—faith, hope, and love—and the dynamic for its actualization. This ethics of the Spirit is the ethics of the church. Even now in our apocalyptic time, the Spirit is moving over the face of the world and through the community of the Spirit God is commanding: "Let there be light" and behold, light breaks forth, and God says, "It is good."

Regarded by a wide spectrum of theological scholars as the major Christian proponent of sanctification, Wesley's union of reform and holiness offers a biblical insight which may become, as it was in his era, the force of a mighty wind. Wherever that wind moves there flows a moral current which shapes the living of this earthly life in all of its commonplaces. Thus the world is being transformed by the real presence of the Spirit of God.

8

THE CHURCH AS AN
ETHICAL COMMUNITY

The Holy Spirit, who is the manifest moral power of God, on the day of Pentecost inaugurated the church of Jesus Christ, the fellowship (*koinonia*) of love. From a study of an ethics of the Spirit we proceed quite naturally to an evaluation of the church as the redemptive ethical fellowship. Wesley's conception of the social nature of the Christian community is the corrective to the argument of critics that his concern was too individual and inadequately social. The church as *koinonia*, however, represents Wesley's best ecclesiology. As a corporate structure, the church is a leavening Christian society in the whole human society, offering a critique of the world order and proposals for effecting moral renewal.

The church in Christian theology has been defined primarily in terms of worship and ethics. Catholic thought has emphasized that the church is one, holy, apostolic, and universal. These terms describe the church's character amplifying communal, ethical, historical, and geographical aspects. When the Reformation creeds were formulated beginning with Augsburg in 1530, the marks of the church were set forth in evangelical and sacramental terms. Preaching the gospel and administering the sacraments take place in the worshiping community, the assembly of believers. Central to the Anabaptist faith was the mark of church discipline. Christian scholars have attributed to Martin Bucer the major articulation of this mark.[1] This is apparently correct in its theoretical development but the Anabaptists surely gave the concept its living sinew in the years from 1525–35.

A fourth Protestant mark is community or *koinonia*. Central to St. Luke's commentary on the early church (Acts 2), this theme is given preeminence in Wesleyan ecclesiology. Such is its prominence that the noted Methodist scholar Gordon Rupp claims that Wesley was the primary theological inspiration for this mark.[2]

It is common in theological conversation to address the significance of the church in preaching and worship. Less frequently seen is the ethical significance of the church. Holiness, however, is an ethical category, demarcating the church's separation from the world. As a community of faith[3] the church is by nature and by definition an ethical community. By example the church models the ethics of Jesus. It is the "city" on the hill exposed to the view of the world, the "salt" that transforms the styles of the age. The church is also a "community of moral discourse,"[4] where reflection concerning the moral claims of Christ's teaching takes place. This is a continuing task. Beginning with the revelatory word of Christ with its pledge of the kingdom, realized now in faith and hope, it continues to address the moral issues present in every age. In both its exemplary and reflective roles, the church performs its task in the empowering and sanctifying work of the Spirit. The Holy Spirit is the reaching out of Christ's presence through the church to the world.

George F. Thomas has described the ethical task of the church as, first, "the fostering of the Christian life of its members through the means of grace it provides," and second, "to stimulate the practice of love in all the relations of Christians to their neighbors *outside the Church*." [5] The church provides a context for moral and spiritual growth, for a deepened sensitivity to the needs of others. The church as "fellowship" is committed to nurture.

The church is marked by love. That Christians often fail to show love does not detract from Christ's mandate. The moral demand of love is to regard every person as neighbor, to avoid partiality, and to act from the motive of concern. Jesus taught that the Christian lifestyle is based upon a new motivation, not the old "eye for an eye." Whenever Christians take their cues from the world's standard of conduct, they become pressed into the world's mold. "Turning the other cheek" is Jesus' metaphor for refusing to shape life by the world's actions. The moral influence of the church is toward conversion or transformation, not accommodation or capitulation. As the community of the Holy Spirit, the church contradicts the world's unholy purposes. As a community of unity, it challenges the world's alienations. As a missionary community it cannot withhold the Good News from all the world. Therefore, it is inevitable that the church and world will live in tension, continually acting and reacting upon each other.

John Wesley portrays the church as a moral community. Analysis of his conception of the church viewed both in ideal and empirical terms, demonstrates that ecclesiological questions are secondary to moral considerations.

His purpose in the Methodist societies was not to raise up a new church, but to reform the nation and the church and to spread scriptural holiness across the land. These goals were to be kept in a parallel relationship. Reformation and holiness were integral concerns. Wesley thought that reform might come through holy living, that wherever this message was proclaimed, moral and spiritual change would take place.[6] Wesley's belief that the Church of England was in sore need of reform shaped his views. The contemporary revival of interest in the primitive church[7] and in its moral power and purity, led Wesley to espouse the early church as a model for his church. He wrote, "I reverence these ancient Christians (with all their failings) more because I see so few Christians now; because I . . . hear so little of genuine Christianity."[8]

THE IDEAL OF THE PRIMITIVE CHURCH

Wesley looked backward to the early church as the ideal by which the church should be measured in every age. He described that early church in the scriptural account in the Acts of the Apostles. So impressed was Wesley with the account (Acts 2–4) that he exulted, "Here was the dawn of the proper Gospel day. Here was a proper Christian Church."[9]

Soon, however, the "mystery of iniquity" began to work. The plague of love for money and partiality infected the church. Partiality was defined as "too much regard for those of our own side; and too little for others, though equally worthy."[10] The church was soon healed of its sickness by persecution. Wesley interpreted the history of the Christian church as a series of alternating moments when righteousness reigned to be succeeded by spiritual decay. Even the first-century church faced this dilemma. Therefore, although Wesley idealized the primitive church, he saw that it, too, felt the tremendous impact of evil.[11] The church in every age faces and feels the power of corruption. No visible church is perfect. Wesley regarded the churches at Smyrna and Philadelphia to be stronger than most visible churches because they possessed less material wealth, but even they did not escape the problem of evil.[12]

In summary, the primitive church possessed unity of spirit and dynamic Christian love. Paradoxically, it also often demonstrated the absence of these graces, falling into sin. Yet, Wesley's usual concept of the primitive church was that of the ideal church acting in love, doing good works, engaged in living fellowship. The primitive church and certain practices attributed to it became models for Wesley in his experience.

Admiring the early church, Wesley possessed a realistic appraisal of it and the Christian church in its historic development. Like Richard Hooker and John Pearson, he interpreted Jesus' parable of the tares to mean that the visible church would have good and evil mixed together.[13] Such figures as wine mixed with water and "evil leaven" expressed his conception of the mixed character of the church. His sermon, "Of the Church," described the dilution that weakened the church. This sermon was much more positive than the gloomy picture presented in the sermon, "The Mystery of Iniquity," described above.

His affection for the primitive church was mirrored in a hymn included in his *Works*,[14] entitled "Primitive Christianity."

> Happy the souls who first believed,
> To Jesus and each other cleaved,
> Joined by the unction from above,
> In mystic fellowship of love!
>
> Meek simple followers of the Lamb
> They lived and spoke and thought the same;
> Brake the commemorative bread
> And drank the Spirit of their Head.
>
> To Jesus they performed their vows;
> A little Church in every house,
> They joyfully conspired to raise
> Their ceaseless sacrifice of praise.
>
> Propriety was there unknown,
> None called what he possessed his own[15]
> Where all the common blessings share,
> No selfish happiness was there.

With grace abundantly endued,
A pure, believing multitude!
They all were of one heart and soul,
And only love inspired the whole.

Where shall I wander now to find
The successors they left behind?
The faithful whom I seek in vain,
Are 'minished from the sons of men.

Ye different sects, who all declare,
"Lo, here is Christ!" or, "Christ is there!"
Your stronger proofs divinely give,
And show me where the Christians live.[16]

Your claim, alas! ye cannot prove,
Ye want the genuine mark of love;
Thou only, Lord, thine own canst show;
For sure thou hast a Church below.

The gates of hell cannot prevail,
The Church on earth can never fail:
Ah! join me to thy secret ones!
Ah! gather all thy living stones!

From this selection of the thirty-verse hymn, it is clear that this pristine church was to Wesley the epitome of the church. He did not see in the church of his own age the marks of love, unity, and purity, which were so luminous in the primitive Christian era.

Other motifs emerge in this hymn, the aspect of hiddeness, of smallness, and of oppression.[17]

The few that truly call thee Lord
And wait thy sanctifying word
And thee their utmost Saviour own,
Unite, and perfect them in one.

Gather them in on every side,
And in thy tabernacle hide;
Give them a resting-place to find,
A covert from the storm and wind.

O find them out some calm recess,
Some unfrequented wilderness;
Thou, Lord, the secret place prepare,
And hide and feed "the woman" there.
In them let all mankind behold
How Christians lived in days of old.

What are the marks of the primitive church? This hymn reiterates the emphases found elsewhere of unity and fellowship, purity, faith, and love. Discussing Acts 5:11, he wrote, "And here is a native specimen of a New Testament church; which is a company of men, called by the gospel, grafted into Christ by baptism, animated by love, united by all kind of fellowship, and disciplined by the death of Ananias and Sapphira."[18]

AN EVANGELICAL CONCEPTION OF THE CHURCH

Wesley was fully aware of the confessional history of the Church of England, expressed particularly in the Thirty-nine Articles. His interpretation of Article 19 is best expressed in his sermon on the church. In this sermon he analyzes the article on the church, stressing its ethical significance above the functional role of the church in preaching the Word of God and administering the sacraments. He focused attention upon the persons who belong to the church. They are marked by their living faith. Wesley recited the nineteenth article: "The visible church of Christ is a congregation of faithful men, in which the pure word of God is preached and the sacraments be duly administered." According to Wesley, when the Articles were published, a Latin translation was prepared using the words *coetus credentium*, a congregation of believers, "plainly showing that by *faithful men*, the compilers meant, men endued with *living faith*." [19] This ethical definition describing the condition of moral and spiritual change, gives attention to the basis of membership in the Christian community. Nevertheless, Wesley takes seriously the relationship between faith, preaching, and the sacraments. Three things are essential to a visible church, he claims:

> First, living faith; without which, indeed, there can be no Church at all, neither visible, nor invisible.
>
> Secondly, preaching and consequently hearing, the pure word of God, else that faith would languish and die. And
>
> Thirdly, a due administration of the sacraments, the ordinary means whereby God increaseth faith.[20]

This deliberate preference of ethical over doctrinal or ecclesiastical criteria pervades the Wesleyan literature. Expounding on Ephesians 4:1–6, Wesley emphasized the character of the church:

> Here . . . is a clear unexceptionable answer to that question, "What is the Church?" The Catholic or universal church is, all the persons in the universe whom God hath so called out of the world as to entitle them to the preceding character; as to be "one body," united by "one Spirit," having "one faith, one hope, one baptism."[21]

The underlying stratum is *persons* who are *called out of the world* with the *character* of *holiness*.

> The Church is called *holy*, because it *is* holy, because every member thereof is holy, though in different degrees, as He that called them is holy. . . . If the Church as to the essence of it is a body of believers, no man that is not a Christian believer can be a member of it.[22]

Wesley leaves no doubt concerning his intention here. By "Christian believer" he means one who has vital, evangelical faith; faith that renews and sanctifies.

Wesley's strong accent upon ethics does not mean that he was careless about the church's doctrine or sacraments. He does question the insistence upon the criterion of preaching the pure word in the Articles, insisting that the church has often existed even where false teaching has been presented.[23] He recognizes that a disjunction between faith as assent and as trust often occurs. The primitive church had many persons who gave evidence of their vital faith while they were confused or heterodox in the faith that the catholic church would eventually adopt. Nevertheless, Wesley was himself orthodox at all points and held no brief for false teaching.

Wesley's lifelong zeal in preaching Christ ("offering Christ"), gives a clear picture of his loyalty to historic faith. His writings stress the "fundamentals," or essentials of the faith, but he was not a Fundamentalist. His "Letter to a Roman Catholic"[24] written in 1749 is thoroughly orthodox, affirming all of the ancient Christian creedal positions.

In summary, evangelical faith is a valid moral category for it expresses the criterion of admission to the church. A believer possesses a new moral relationship, for faith is the door to life. The believer experiences a new world in Christ (2 Cor. 5:17). Expressed differently, Wesley would insist that the church is comprised of persons "called out of the world." A new spirit

motivates the believer, making the Christian live in a relationship of tension with the world.

THE CHURCH AS A HOLY COMMUNITY

Evangelical faith opens up and sets in process the life of
holiness. Holiness is the moral opposite of proud self-
sufficiency, for holiness is the imaging of God in us.

Albert C. Knudsen, one of the theologians of the Boston
University "personalist" school, writes:

> Holiness . . . is inherent in the life and faith of the church.
> The church is a regenerated body of believers, and as such, a
> symbol and pledge of a redeemed and perfected society. . . .
> Thus viewed the church is in its essential nature an ethical
> institution. . . . It exists as the bearer of the Christian moral
> ideal and as the medium through which this ideal is to be
> realized.[25]

Holiness is regarded by Wesley as the lifelong process in
which God is modeling us in increasing conformity to this life.
Using the analogy of a house, he describes repentance as the
porch and faith as the door to the dwelling. Repentance and
faith are the indispensable preparations for holiness. Faith is
the handmaiden of love.[26] However, Wesley has no intention to
suggest that faith may be abandoned once love is experienced.
Faith and love are linked in vital, organic unity.

The tendency in traditional Catholic theology is to view the
institutional church as holy. Recognizing the flaws of individual
church members, and even popes, the church's teaching fathers
consider the institution holy because it is Christ's church.

Wesley, in common with Protestant thinkers, emphasizes
the holiness of those who constitute the church; believers who
are called out of the world to emulate the sanctity of the God
who called them. The church is holy because the persons who
believe are holy.

Most students of Christian history are aware that Wesley is
one of the greatest exponents of Christian holiness. What
Luther is to justification by faith, and Calvin is to the
sovereignty of God, Wesley is to sanctification. Appreciation for
his particular interpretation is mixed, from zealous partisanship
to fierce opposition. Many of those persons who live within the
ecclesiastical context he established, Methodism and its many
branches, acknowledge his genius for his era but regard his

teachings as dusty archaisms.[27] Wesley theologians are described as an "endangered species."[28]

Wesley's concern for a life lived in righteousness is of massive significance in the church's confrontation with culture. His approach to culture has not been adequately assessed, but he is by no means committed to a pie-in-the-sky perspective. Holiness is lived out in society where alienated persons live and where the Christian message brings healing.

Culture may be characterized as always social, human achievement; it is concerned with temporal and material realization of values, and is pluralistic.[29] Believing that every human effort is flawed by man's rebellion, Wesley cannot uncritically affirm the social order. However, Wesley's pessimism is overcome by an optimism of grace. He is convinced that culture may be transformed, not by any earthly kingdom, but by Christ's future kingdom, which casts its light over the present. Christian holiness is the proleptic[30] realization of the coming kingdom. In Christ, a new life begins, a holy life, which anticipates the kingdom. In the hope of that kingdom, believers purify themselves (1 John 3:1); they are perfect as the Father is perfect (Matt. 5:48). As those who are made holy in love, having a foretaste of glory, they bring Christ's kingdom into the ways of the earthly community. The result is tension between two kingdoms, but also transformation; hostility but reconciliation; anger, but peace. When the church no longer partakes the life of God, when faith is form without life, then the world's invasion of the church creates the state of conformity. Now the kingdoms of time have lost the salting power of the kingdom of heaven.

When Wesley taught that Christians ought to press on into the perfection of love, he sought at least two ends. First, that the spirit of evil might be conquered in the believer's life, that the love of the world might be succeeded by the love of God. Second, that the love of God might prepare the believer to love the world in order to redeem the world. By using physical analogies drawn particularly from the Augustinian and Reformed views of man as sinner, Wesley gave support to a "substantial" conception of sin and sanctification. If sin is an inherited substance ("inbred sin"), then radical surgery ("circumcision of the heart") is the appropriate metaphor by which to describe deliverance. This description of the problem often leads to a private, personal, and individualistic solution. Among the holiness people, where it received its flowering in the post-Civil War era and in the early decades of this century, it tended to express itself in a world-denying lifestyle. Too often it was private, churchly holiness rather than the world-trans-forming force of Wesleyan "social holiness."

Another side to this coin may be found in Wesley's thought. Robert E. Chiles, Harald Lindström, and John Peters assert that Wesley views sin and salvation more in terms of sickness and health, and as a distortion of relationships. Chiles states his interpretation of Wesley, "Sin is not so much ontological degradation or demolition of human reality as it is illness or contagion; not so much biological and subpersonal distortion, as it is an inversion of relationships involving motive and intention."[31]

The implication of a relational interpretation is a greater congeniality for social ethics. The private, personal sphere is not overlooked or diminished by this theological emphasis. Christ's redemptive love is as much relative to me as it is to my relation to God and neighbor. However, the relational focus prevents an overweening preoccupation with self, with the quality and condition of the inner life. In Christ, new life not only includes the self but it includes others. A theology that fails to accent this command of love must become narrow in its teaching. To define sin and salvation in relational terms places the emphasis where it belongs, upon sin as personal and social. A believer must come to terms with the double-edged character of sin.

Here the emphasis is placed upon the healing of our relationship to God and man. There is no denial of the awful estrangement of man from God. James Arminius, for example, held a Reformed conception of sinful humanity, but he was convinced that the essence of sin should be described as the absence of the Holy Spirit, a relational concept. Arminius avoided the concept "original sin" or depravity, preferring to describe man's sinful life as privation. But isn't there more than the absence of good? Arminius's response was, "We think it much more probable that this absence of original righteousness, only, is original sin itself, as being that which alone is sufficient to commit and produce any actual sins."[32] The logic of Arminius is that if the Fall is the privation of the Spirit, then salvation means the restoration of that same Spirit. This is in line with Paul's teaching on the "renewal of the Spirit."

Some interpreters of Wesley will prefer the "substantial" concept of sin and holiness, while others will follow the

Wesleyan concern that emphasizes the restored relationship of love. Love, not the cleansing of sin, is the *goal* of Christ's work. Love cannot be perfect where the believer is conformed to sin. Nevertheless, deliverance from sin is for Wesley but a stage along life's way to love. Wesley's great vision is the biblical vision that Christians may love God and man in the wholeness of God's perfectness. No completion of this pilgrimage is to be found in the earthly life. Christian holiness is an ascent of the mountain of God that will not be finished until the believer is with Christ. The mountain and the ascent are real. In faith, hope, and love, the faraway goal is made vital to the one who is being conformed to Christ.

The holy church is characterized by love. In the hymn "Primitive Christianity," Wesley seeks for the genuine Christian: "Show me where the Christians live!" He writes, "Your claim, alas, ye cannot prove. Ye want the genuine mark of love!"[33] In his hymn on religious tolerance, Wesley amplifies his desire for a holy church:

> Let others draw, with fierce despite,
>   The eradicating sword,
> And with the devil's weapons fight
>   The battles of the Lord.
>
> But, O! my gracious God, to me
>   A better spirit impart;
> The gentle mind that was in thee,
>   The meekly loving heart.[34]

THE CHURCH AS *KOINONIA* IN HUMAN COMMUNITY

For Wesley, Christianity is social in nature and consistently expresses its unique character in social interaction. There appear to be two major aspects or functions of the church that amplify its social character: first, the uniting for fellowship with other true believers within the small group for mutual encouragement and edification; second, the functioning of believers within the larger society or community—the aspect of mission. It is the concept of the church as a society of believers engaging in mission within the larger society, the civil or secular society. The church realizes itself in the community of believers and gives demonstration of itself as a spiritual society operating in the larger society. Wesley's unequivocal statement concerning the social character of the gospel of Christ amplifies this assertion.[35]

The concept of the church as a society or community united for fellowship, is a definite part of Wesley's ecclesiology. Williams has made the important point that for Wesley, *koinonia* is a special word meaning, "holding things in common."[36] The primitive church did not share in this commonalty as a response to a temporary need, but because it was the expression of an overflowing love for each other; it was true fellowship. Wesley described the glorious church that appeared at Pentecost, the unity of heart and mind present, and the fellowship. "In *fellowship;* this is, having all things in common; no man counting anything he had his own."[37] The "happy state" described here did not last because the love of money engendered discord.

The church as community is best expressed by Wesley in three sermons, "Catholic Spirit," "Upon Our Lord's Sermon on the Mount," and "God's Vineyard."[38] The rules of the United Societies provide further insight. These sermons and rules enunciate the concept of fellowship and the concept of mission, the role of the society of Christians within the world.

Wesley at various times uses the terms *church* and *society* synonymously.[39] Evidently he uses *society* in a restricted sense to refer to a particular, or local church, a branch of the universal church. The Christian ought to be zealous for the church, praying both for the universal church and for the "particular Church or Christian society whereof he . . . is a member."[40] Discussing baptism with the Baptist, Gilbert Boyce, Wesley assured him of his persuasion that neither Methodists nor the Church of England could be considered the *"True Church of Christ.* For that Church is but one, and contains all the true believers on earth. But I conceive every society of true believers to be a branch of the one true Church of Christ."[41] However, though the concept of universal church is present in Wesley's thought, he generally appeared to be more concerned about the society of believers who make up the particular church, or "society," and their positive zeal in demonstrating Christian love. Using the figure of a conical or circular hierarchy with Christian love at the apex, Wesley enunciated a concept of Christians united in fellowship and work, in holy tempers, works of mercy, works of piety, all exercised and realized through the church, universal and particular. These circles begin on the lowest level with the assembling of Christians together and rise one above another to the summit, "love enthroned in the heart." Christian zeal should be exercised for the assembled church, but the greatest zeal should be reserved for Christian love, love for God and all mankind. Wesley's intent here is to show that the Christian society is not an end in itself, but a means to greater love. Union with a Christian society was an excellent support for the development of Christian grace, particularly love.[42]

Wesley expressed in many ways his concern for the involvement of the individual in the spiritual community and the civil community. Vigorously opposing the quietism of the mystical writers,[43] he declared that Christians could not live in isolation from others. Holiness can only be developed in communion with the holy society of believers. Solitary religion is not found in the gospel of Christ. The solitary Christian cannot possibly be merciful, taking every opportunity to do good to all.[44]

This aspect of Wesley's teaching means involvement in the Christian society or community. But it can by no means be limited to the saints. For the society of which Wesley speaks is the worldly society of those who do not know God. There is fellowship to be shared even with the wicked person who is a citizen in the same world in which the Christian lives. Separation from the world will result in the forfeiture of the faith. The only way that the Christian can realize the expectations of Christ's kingdom, the exercise of meekness and peacemaking, is through relationships with the world. The ideals of the Sermon on the Mount are achieved amidst everyday contacts with the world. Yet, this contact is by no means merely for improvement of the Christian. Christians are placed among other persons by the providence of God, "that whatever grace you have received of God may through you be communicated to others; that every holy temper and word and work of yours may have an influence on them also."[45]

Wesley believed that true religion lives within the heart. True religion is summed up in Christian love, and although no outward form can possibly replace this root characteristic, the presence of the root will mean the growth of branches. Love does not supersede faith or good works, but arises from faith and pours forth good works.[46] Whether the Christian is moving within the small fellowship of believers or the larger fellowship of mankind, love is the controlling force. The former assists in the nourishing of love, while the latter provides an object of need on which Christian charity may be bestowed and amidst which it can be put to the test of endurance and validity.[47]

As previously noted, Rupp argues that, with Wesley, a fourth dimension, or mark, of the church comes into prominence alongside the historic emphasis on Word, sacrament, and discipline. The importance of the church as community is now recognized, especially the idea of the "Christian cell."[48] Rupp's claim seems to give inadequate attention to the important precedents set by the Pietists, the Anabaptists, and the Moravians. Certainly Wesley approved of this perspective, as we have seen. It is clear that Wesley's concept of church society or community is to be understood as a society or community operative in the larger society—the true church leavening the society called the world. It is not individual Christians so much as Christians united in fellowship, engaging the total worldly society in works of mercy and love. These works are by no means just the saving of souls, but always the healing of lives, restoring hope to hungry, sick, impoverished men. It is the balanced synthesis of social action and spiritual renewal. The Word, sacraments, discipline, and the community of believers are given in order that faith may bring forth love. Assembling in church with fellow Christians is purposeful, that faith might be created, and faith is always the handmaid of love. Love always involves the divine and human spheres. "Thou shalt love the Lord thy God. . . .; and thy neighbour . . . ," was Wesley's consistent, microcosmic definition of Christian perfection. Love as a mark of the church is essential to Wesley's view of the church, even as it is essential to his view of religious toleration.

The Wesleyan concept of the Christian society working within the larger society is expressed in the sermon, "Catholic Spirit."[49] By "catholic spirit," Wesley means love; "catholic love is a catholic spirit." It is this love for God and man that causes Christians to unite in fellowship. Wesley acknowledged that external union might not be realistic because persons disagree on questions of theology or worship; but that they would unite in a community of Christians he had no doubt: "Every follower of Christ is obliged, by the very nature of the Christian institution, to be a member of some particular congregation or other."[50] That congregation is one that is chosen by the Christian, without coercion.

From this community, the believer's love is extended beyond to the larger Christian and non-Christian society.

Wesley asks not for unanimity of opinion but of love. If Christian love is expressed toward friend or foe; if love is demonstrated by good works toward even the enemies of God; if a sincere effort is made to supply their "wants," giving assistance in body and soul, in spiritual or temporal matters; opinions may vary. That a special kind of love is owed to those who love God is certain, but the "royal law" causes love for all mankind to flow from the believing soul.[51] In summary then, Wesley argues that Christianity is a social religion that draws Christ's followers into a social relationship, first with fellow believers, then the larger civil society. There is something special in the former relationship that marks it off from the fellowship of unbelieving persons, but this demarcation is a thing of commitment. The body of believers, according to Christ's "royal law," will be drawn out into the world to assist in the healing of body and spirit, the development of temporal and spiritual. This union of believing souls that precedes the identification with human needs in the world, becomes a pattern in the structure of the Methodist societies. The rules of the United Societies are the verbalized expectations which he laid upon his members, growing out of his socially oriented concept of the Christian's responsibility in his total life context. The rules spell out both the concept of fellowship and mission, fellowship in the small community, mission in and to the larger.[52]

9

EPILOGUE:
The Promise of Wesley's Ethics

Long neglected as a source for serious theological discourse, Wesley's theology has been gaining increasing understanding and appreciation. His ethical contributions have not been borne along by this interest, but some have been seeking to trace the historical lines of Wesley's influence upon the life and morals of his land. Maldwyn Edward's writings have demonstrated the impact of Methodism on the eighteenth century[1] and Wellman Warner has studied the influence of the Wesleyan revival on the industrial revolution. [2]

Elie Halevy's controversial thesis continues to attract the attention of students of the Wesleyan era. Asserting that the Wesleyan revival sublimated, or redirected, the social energies of a disaffected citizenry away from poverty and unemployment toward spiritual goals, Halevy argued that the potential for a French-style English Revolution was defused. Bernard Semmel has assessed this hypothesis in an introductory essay, but intensive work is required before an adequate scholarly response may be offered.[3]

Wesley receives occasional notice in discussions of the Protestant ethic initiated by Max Weber and developed by R. H. Tawney. Wesley's economic ethic is sharply critical of affluence and most sympathetic to the poor. His view of Christian stewardship leads him to oppose surplus accumulation in a needy world. The apparent contrast between Adam Smith's laissez-faire economics and Wesley's incipient appeal for some form of social and economic regulation should be analyzed carefully.

In a world where political totalitarianism is increasing and where radicalism is threatening both Eastern and Western society, Wesley's appeal for a state ordered (placed) under God and his commitment to human freedom needs to be heard again. His concern for human values is as pertinent in our times as it was in his.

In the continuing and ever more urgent search for ethical guidance, Wesley's ethics holds great promise. In final illustration, an important case study may be found in his "Thoughts Upon Slavery" issued in 1774. Wesley's essay borrows extensively from a tract written by the American Quaker Anthony Benezet.[4] It contains a significant appeal for human values and brotherhood. Significant principles enunciate the appeal to human freedom, based upon both the will of the Creator and the "Crown Rights of the Redeemer."[5] These principles are noted and applied to issues that are continually contemporary.

First, human freedom is as much a necessity as breathing, and is the privilege of every person born into the world. It is rooted in the divine order and is not subject to human caprice. God in His wisdom has set humanity in the total order of His creation, and that order does not permit the enslavement of some in the service of others. To hold another person in slavery means self-enslavement; the inevitable demeaning and depersonalization of both the enslaved and the enslaver. It is to set up the structures of confrontation and rebellion, for it is to be expected that persons possessing the ontological status of free beings will express that inherent sense. Those who are burdened by oppression will find ways to break out. No one can stop the surging strength of freedom.

The experience of European and American slavery is filled with examples of rebellion against oppression—sometimes psychological, sometimes religious, sometimes physical. Wesley argued that the rebellion of slaves was an expression of the basic God-given right to liberty.

Second, every person without respect to race is entitled to the guarantees of law. Kipling referred arrogantly to the "lesser breeds without the law." The slave trade and the slavery institution was regarded as perfectly legal and acceptable. However, the black person, "without the law," lived under the superior law of the Creator. God's law preempts and judges each expression of human law. There is a higher law, as Wesley, Gilbert Haven, and the proponents of civil disobedience have often declared. That law is to be heard and obeyed, even if it means the breaking of human legislation. Wesley wrote, "Notwithstanding ten thousand laws right is right, and wrong is wrong." One may not enslave any person on the basis of race or any other appeal. God's law has decreed the right to live in freedom.

This decree is preeminently illustrated in the Exodus of Israel. "Let *my* people go that they may serve *me,* " God commanded Pharaoh. The words "my" and "me" are noteworthy, stressing the service of God above that of Pharaoh.

Third, human, values—life, liberty, and happiness—so often subordinated to political goals and ambitions, are more to be treasured than national glory. Wesley lived at the heart of England's drive to become the greatest colonial power in history. The glory of the empire, however, was gained at the expense of many personal and social values both in England and in the empire. While Wesley would never know the impact of imperial England on India or the Middle East, he was informed on the abuses of slavery in Africa and in the British colonies in the West Indies. Wesley was a dedicated citizen, but he declared that it were better for empire to cease than that expansion be made at the expense of enslaved persons.

There are some serious implications to be extrapolated from this judgment. If national self-interest is not an adequate rationale for the denial of human rights, rarely, if ever, may institutional or individual gains be justified at the expense of civil or religious liberties.

Wesley insisted on the right to a good and decent life. With so many poor in his society, he sought by personal benevolence and by raising support in his Methodist societies to assist the poor. More than this, he spoke to politicians and his countrymen on their responsibility to care. Although he preceded the industrial revolution, his expressed concerns for the poor and the helpless leave us no doubt whose cause he would espouse in the dislocations of the industrial age.

Fourth, the rights of men and women are eviscerated when the full benefits of education and religion are withheld. There were those who charged blacks with ignorance and wickedness. Wesley declared that this was precisely the fault of slaveholders who denied the benefits of education and Christian faith to them. Their presumed ignorance was simply a cultural factor and not intellectual density. In their own milieu, they were equal or superior to their white captors. If they were to function intelligently in a new world, they must be offered opportunity to learn. They surely had been educated to live in their native environs. Once more the issue is opportunity. Further, they must hear the Good News of the gospel in order for their wickedness to be overcome. Deprive any person of freedom—freedom to move within normal restraints; freedom to develop basic intellectual gifts and social graces; freedom to accept and follow the Word of Christ—and that person will be forced into a position of confrontation, despair, and hopelessness. No wonder, wrote Wesley, that the blacks rebelled. Their behavior was being determined to a great degree by the conflict of natural right with the imposed law of despotic slave lords.

The same issues prevail in our era. No one expects that it will be simple to solve the problems in a complex society. Nevertheless, unless the essentials of the good life, ordained by the Author of the law of nature, are opened up to the many, without prejudice of class or race, the society will foster a constellation of responses that will be damaging to the entire society. Freedom to learn and to achieve, the right to follow conscience in matters of religion—these are woven into the universe of man and may no more be ignored than the law of gravity.

Fifth, freedom from respect for persons may be realized in the biblical principle of human brotherhood. Wesley's firm persuasion that blacks and whites are brothers was voiced in his recollection of God's ancient word to Cain. After Cain had assumed a prerogative that only God could claim, the taking of life, God said, "The voice of thy brother's blood crieth . . . from the ground" (Gen. 4:10 KJV). Wesley cited this passage in the defense of murdered and brutalized black men. Slave owners had seen blacks as chattels. Wesley saw them as brothers. He wrote, " 'The blood of thy brother' (for whether thou wilt believe it or no, such he is in the sight of Him that made him) 'crieth against thee from the earth.' "[6]

Wesley appealed to the human character of the slaveholder. Treating other human beings as slaves is to reduce oneself to a level of the animals that prey on the helpless. "Whether you are a Christian or no, show yourself a man! Be not more savage than a lion or a bear!"

To regard someone as a brother means to recognize his humanity. This leads to acknowledgment of human rights—choice, movement, respect, reciprocity. The appeal to brotherhood, for Wesley, means banishment of slavery and the inauguration of freedom with all its egalitarian implications. Wesley did not envision the outcome of all these implications, but he espoused principles contributing to their fulfillment. No reservation to the full development of human potential may be retained. Every person's honor, dignity, and self-expression are of central significance.

Wesley concluded his tract by asserting God's love to all, that God is the Father of all; God's concern for the oppressed, that God is both Creator *and* Savior of these captives. He prays for the Lord to create within them a cry for freedom that will rise up to the ears of the Almighty; that there might be an "Exodus" in the age of the Englightment that would free these people of God. In fact he specifically alludes to the restoration of the Babylon exiles as he paraphrases Psalm 126:4—"turn their captivity as the rivers in the south"—and applies this passage to the freedom of the blacks. That Wesley saw the liberation of the slave as being in continuity with the Exodus event and the release of the exiles from Babylon seems clear.

Themes like those in "Thoughts Upon Slavery" abound in Wesley's writings, especially in the last three decades of his life. All of the stereotypes of Wesley's political and social views lead us to expect little instruction from him toward solving the stresses of modern society. His vision seems to many like an idyllic dream of Paradise, but few modern men or women have reflected so *realistically and yet hopefully* upon the human prospect.

This essay ends on the same note where it began— promise. Wesley's realistic assessment of human nature is sustained by all of the empirical evidence discovered in a lonely, lost generation. Nevertheless, sin is not the dominant note. The triumph of grace is never obscured by human depravity. Grace still illuminates the darkening skies of our age. Dr. Starkey's summation superbly expresses Wesley's theology:

> John Wesley's understanding of the Christian life in terms of God's possibilities rather than man's incapacities; of, God's promises rather than man's fears; of God's victorious presence *here* and *now* in the Holy Spirit for guidance, comfort and strength, rather than in some future age; needs to be reasserted today.[7]

This review of Wesley's theological foundations for ethical inquiry attempts to open to a larger audience the promise of Wesley's ethics. Balancing his profound understanding of biblical faith with an uncommon astuteness in observing England and its people for eighty-seven years (1703–1791), Wesley's Christian ethics is an "ethics of hope" for real people in a real world. The early Methodists sang jubilantly their hope of a new world, free from the infinite varieties of human anguish:

> Messiah, Prince of God!
>   Where men each other tear,
> Where war is learn'd they must confess
>   Thy kingdom is not there.
> Who, prompted by thy foe,
>   Delight in human blood,
> Apollyon is their king, we know,
>   And Satan is their god.
>
> But shall he still devour
>   The souls redeem'd by thee?
> Jesus, stir up thy glorious power,
>   And end the apostasy!
> Come, Saviour from above,
>   O'er all our hearts to reign;
> And plant the kingdom of thy love
>   In every heart of man.
>
> Then shall we exercise
>   The hellish art no more,
> While thou, our long-lost paradise,
>   Dost with thyself restore
> Fightings and wars shall cease
>   And, in thy Spirit given,
> Pure joy and everlasting peace,
>   Shall turn our earth to heaven.[8]

APPENDIX
SERMON: "THE REFORMATION OF MANNERS"

This sermon was preached by Wesley on January 30, 1763 before The Society for Reformation of Manners. It reflects some of Wesley's perceptions on the criteria for those who would be public reformers. The excerpt contained here does not typify Wesley's approach to reform but it does suggest a strategy, somewhat similar to that of Calvin at Geneva, that deals with the suppression of evil and the reformation of society. Wesley's discussion of the characteristics of the reformer suggests an uncommon quality of redemptive motivation modeled by the reformer.

"Who will rise up with me against the wicked?" — Ps. 94:16.

1. In all ages, men who neither feared God nor regarded man have combined together, and formed confederacies, to carry on the works of darkness. And herein they have shown themselves wise in their generation; for by this means they more effectually promoted the kingdom of their father the devil, than otherwise they could have done. On the other hand, men who did fear God, and desire the happiness of their fellow creatures, have, in every age, found it needful to join together, in order to oppose the works of darkness, to spread the knowledge of God their Saviour, and to promote His kingdom upon earth. Indeed He Himself has instructed them so to do. From the time that men were upon the earth, He hath taught them to join together in His service, and has united them in one body by one Spirit. And for this very end He had joined them together, 'that He might destroy the works of the devil'; first in them that are already united, and by them in all that are round about them.

2. This is the original design of the church of Christ. It is a body of men compacted together, in order, first to save each his own soul; then to assist each other in working out their salvation; and, afterwards, as far as in them lies, to save all men from present and future misery, to overturn the kingdom of Satan, and set up the kingdom of Christ. And this ought to be the continued care and

endeavour of every member of His Church; otherwise he is not worthy to be called a member thereof, as he is not a living member of Christ.

3. Accordingly, this ought to be the constant care and endeavour of all those who are united together in these kingdoms, and are commonly called, "The Church of England." They are united together for this very end, to oppose the devil and all his works, and to wage war against the world and the flesh, his constant and faithful allies. But do they in fact, answer the end of their union? Are all who style themselves 'members of the Church of England' heartily engaged in opposing the works of the devil, and fighting against the world and the flesh? Alas! we cannot say this. So far from it, that a great part, I fear the greater part of them, are themselves "the world,"—the people that know not God to any saving purpose; are indulging, day by day, instead of 'mortifying, the flesh, with its affections and desires'; and doing, themselves, those works of the devil, which they are peculiarly engaged to destroy.

4. There is, therefore, still need, even in this Christian country (as we *courteously* style Great Britain), yea, in this Christian Church (if we may give that title to the bulk of our nation), of some to 'rise up against the wicked,' and join together 'against the evil doers.' Nay, there was never more need than there is at this day for them 'that fear the Lord to speak often together' on this very head, how they may 'lift up a standard against the iniquity' which overflows the land. There is abundant cause for all the servants of God to join together against the works of the devil; with united hearts and counsels and endeavours to make a stand for God, and to repress, as much as in them lies, these 'floods of ungodliness.'

5. For this end a few persons in London, towards the close of the last century united together, and, after a while, were termed, *The Society for Reformation of Manners;* and incredible good was done by them for near forty years. But then, most of the original members being gone to their reward, those who succeeded them grew faint in their mind, and departed from the work: so that a few years ago the Society ceased; nor did any of the kind remain in the kingdom.

6. It is a Society of the same nature which has been lately formed. I purpose to show, first, the nature of their design, and the steps they have hitherto taken: secondly, the excellency of it; with the various objections which have been raised against it: thirdly, what manner of men they ought to be who engage in such a design: and, fourthly, with what spirit, and in what manner, they should proceed in the prosecution of it. I shall conclude with an application both to them, and to all that fear God.

III. 1. But what manner of men ought they to be who engage in such a design? Some may imagine, any that are willing to assist therein ought readily to be admitted; and that the greater the number of members, the greater will be their influence. But this is by no means true: matter of fact undeniably proves the contrary. While the former Society for Reformation of Manners consisted of chosen members only, though neither many, rich, nor powerful, they broke through all opposition, and were eminently successful in every branch of their undertaking; but when a number of men less carefully chosen were received into that Society, they grew less and less useful, till, by insensible degrees, they dwindled into nothing.

2. The number, therefore, of the members is no more to be attended to than the riches or eminence. This is a work of God. It is undertaken in the name of God, and for His sake. It follows, that men who neither love nor fear God have no part or lot in this matter. 'Why takest thou My covenant in thy mouth?'

may God say to any of these; 'whereas thou' thyself 'hatest to be reformed, and hast cast My words behind thee.' Whoever, therefore, lives in any known sin is not fit to engage in reforming sinners: more especially if he is guilty, in any instance, or in the least degree, of profaning the name of God; or buying, selling, or doing any unnecessary work on the Lord's day; or offending in any other of those instances which this Society is peculiarly designed to reform. No; let none who stands himself in need of this reformation presume to meddle with such an undertaking. First let him 'pull the beam out of his own eye': let him be himself *unblamable* in all things.

3. Not that this will suffice: every one engaging herein should be more than a harmless man. He should be a man of faith; having, at least, such a degree of that 'evidence of things not seen,' as to aim 'not at the things that are seen, which are temporal, but at those that are not seen, which are eternal'; such faith as produces a steady fear of God, with a lasting resolution, by His grace, to abstain from all that He has forbidden, and to do all that He has commanded. He will more especially need that particular branch of faith,— confidence in God. It is this faith which 'removes mountains'; which 'quenches the violence of fire'; which breaks through all opposition; and enables one to stand against and 'chase a thousand,' knowing in whom his strength lies, and, even when he has the 'sentence of death in himself, trusting in Him who raiseth the dead.'

4. He that has faith and confidence in God will, of consequence, be a man of courage. And such it is highly needful every man should be, who engages in this undertaking: for many things will occur in the prosecution thereof which are terrible to nature; indeed, so terrible, that all who 'confer with flesh and blood' will be afraid to encounter them. Here, therefore, true courage has its proper place, and is necessary in the highest degree. And this faith only can supply. A believer can say,

> I fear no denial, no danger I fear,
> Nor start from the trial, for Jesus is near.

5. To courage patience is nearly allied; the one regarding future, the other present evils. And whoever joins in carrying on a design of this nature, will have great occasion for this. For, notwithstanding all his unblamableness, he will find himself just in Ishmael's situation, 'his hand against every man, and every man's hand against him.' And no wonder: if it be true, that "all who will live godly shall suffer persecution,' how eminently must this be fulfilled in them who, not content to live godly themselves, compel the ungodly to do so too, or, at least, to refrain from notorious ungodliness! Is not this declaring war against all the world? setting all the children of the devil at defiance? And will not Satan himself, 'the prince of this world, the ruler of the darkness' thereof, exert all his subtilty and all his force in support of his tottering kingdom? Who can expect the roaring lion will tamely submit to have the prey plucked out of his teeth? 'Ye have,' therefore, 'need of patience; that, after ye have done the will of God, ye may receive the promise.'

6. And ye have need of steadiness, that ye may 'hold fast' this 'profession of your faith without wavering.' This also should be found in all that unite in this Society; which is not a task for a 'double-minded man'—for one that is 'unstable in his ways.' He that is as a reed shaken with the wind is not fit for this warfare; which demands a firm purpose of soul, a constant, determined resolution. One that is wanting in this may 'set his hand to the plough'; but how soon will he 'look back'! He may, indeed, 'endure for a time; but when

persecution, or tribulation,' public or private troubles, arise, because of the work, 'immediately he is offended.'

7. Indeed, it is hard for any to persevere in so unpleasing a work, unless love overpowers both pain and fear. And, therefore, it is highly expedient, that all engaged therein have 'the love of God shed abroad in their hearts'; that they should all be able to declare, 'We love Him, because He first loved us.' The presence of Him whom their soul loveth will then make their labour light. They can then say, not from the wildness of a heated imagination, but with the utmost truth and soberness,—

> With Thee conversing, I forget
> All time, and toil, and care:
> Labour is rest, and pain is sweet,
> While Thou, my God, are here.

8. What adds a still greater sweetness, even to labour and pain, is the Christian 'love of our neighbour.' When they 'love their neighbour,' that is, every soul of man, 'as themselves,' as their own souls; when 'the love of Christ constrains' them to love one another, 'even as He loved us'; when, as He 'tasted death for every man,' so they are 'ready to lay down their life for their brethren' (including in that number every man, every soul for which Christ died); what prospect of danger will then be able to fright them from their 'labour of love'? What suffering will they not be ready to undergo, to save one soul from everlasting burnings? What continuance of labour, disappointment, pain, will vanquish their fixed resolution? Will they not be—

> 'Gainst all repulses steel'd, nor ever tired
> With toilsome day or ill-succeeding night?

So love both 'hopeth' and 'endureth all things'; so 'charity never faileth.'

9. Love is necessary for all the members of such a Society, on another account likewise; even because 'it is not puffed up'; it produces not only courage and patience, but humility. And O how needful is this for all who are so employed! What can be of more importance, than that they should be little, and mean, and base, and vile, in their own eyes! For, otherwise, should they think themselves anything, should they impute anything to themselves, should they admit anything of a Pharisaic spirit, 'trusting in themselves that they are righteous, and despising others'; nothing could more directly tend to overthrow the whole design. For then they would not only have all the world, but also God Himself, to contend with; seeing He 'resisteth the proud, and giveth grace' only 'to the humble.' Deeply conscious, therefore, should every member of this Society be of his own foolishness, weakness, helplessness; continually hanging, with his whole soul, upon Him who alone hath wisdom and strength, with an unspeakable conviction that 'the help which is done upon earth, God doeth it Himself'; and that it is He alone who 'worketh in us both to will and to do of His good pleasure.'

10. One point more whoever engages in this design should have deeply impressed on his heart; namely, that 'the wrath of man worketh not the righteousness of God.' Let him, therefore, learn of Him who was meek, as well as lowly; and let him abide in meekness, as well as humility: 'with all lowliness and meekness,' let him 'walk worthy of the vocation wherewith he is called.' Let him be 'gentle toward all men,' good or bad, for his own sake, for their sake, for Christ's sake. Are any 'ignorant, and out of the way'? Let him have

'compassion' upon them. Do they even oppose the word and work of God, yea, set themselves in battle array against it? So much the more hath he need 'in meekness to instruct those who thus oppose themselves'; if haply they may 'escape out of the snare of the devil,' and no more be 'taken captive at his will.'

IV. 1. From the qualifications of those who are proper to engage in such an undertaking as this, I proceed to show, fourthly, with what spirit, and in what manner, it ought to be pursued. First, with what spirit. Now this first regards the *motive*, which is to be preserved in every step that is taken; for if, at any time, 'the light which is in thee be darkness, how great is that darkness! But if thine eye be single, thy whole body shall be full of light.' This is, therefore, continually to be remembered, and carried into every word and action. Nothing is to be spoke or done, either great or small, with a view to any temporal advantage; nothing with a view to the favour or esteem, the love or the praise, of men. But the intention, the eye of the mind, is always to be fixed on the glory of God and good of man.

2. But the spirit with which everything is to be done regards the *temper* as well as the motive. And this is no other than that which has been described above. For the same courage, patience, steadiness, which qualify a man for the work, are to be exercised therein. Above all, let him 'take the shield of faith': this will quench a thousand fiery darts. Let him exert all the faith which God has given him, in every trying hour. And let all his doings be done in love: never let this be wrested from him. Neither must many waters quench this love, nor the floods of ingratitude drown it. Let, likewise, that lowly mind be in him which was also in Christ Jesus; yea, and let him 'be clothed with humility,' filling his heart, and adorning his whole behaviour. At the same time, let him 'put on bowels of mercies, gentleness, long-suffering'; avoiding the least appearance of malice, bitterness, anger, or resentment; knowing it is our calling, not to be 'overcome of evil, but to overcome evil with good.' In order to preserve this humble, gentle love, it is needful to do all things with recollection of spirit; watching against all hurry, or dissipation of thought, as well as against pride, wrath, or surliness. But this can be no otherwise preserved than by 'continuing instant in prayer,' both before and after he comes into the field, and during the whole action; and by doing all in the spirit of sacrifice, offering all to God through the Son of His love.

3. As to the outward manner of acting, a general rule is, Let it be expressive of these inward tempers. But, to be more particular: let every man beware not to 'do evil that good may come.' Therefore, 'putting away all lying, let every man speak the truth to his neighbour.' Use no fraud or guile, either in order to detect or to punish any man; but 'by simplicity and godly sincerity commend yourself to men's consciences in the sight of God.' It is probable that, by your adhering to these rules, fewer offenders will be convicted; but so much the more will the blessing of God accompany the whole undertaking.

4. But let innocence be joined with prudence, properly so called: not that offspring of hell which the world calls prudence, which is mere craft, cunning, dissimulation; but with that 'wisdom from above' which our Lord peculiarly recommends to all who would promote His Kingdom upon earth: 'Be ye therefore wise as serpents,' while ye are 'harmless as doves.' This wisdom will instruct you how to suit your words, and whole behaviour, to the persons with whom you have to do; to the time, place, and all other circumstances. It will teach you to cut off occasion of offence, even from those who seek occasion, and to do things of the most offensive nature in the least offensive manner that is possible.

5. Your manner of speaking, particularly to offenders, should be at all times deeply serious (lest it appear like insulting or triumphing over them), rather inclining to sad; showing that you pity them for what they do, and sympathize with them in what they suffer. Let your air and tone of voice, as well as words, be dispassionate, calm, mild; yea, where it would not appear like dissimulation, even kind and friendly. In some cases, where it will probably be received as it is meant, you may profess the goodwill you bear them; but, at the same time (that it may not be thought to proceed from fear, or any wrong inclination), professing your intrepidity, and inflexible resolution to oppose and punish vice to the uttermost.

NOTES

PREFACE

[1]John Wesley, *Works*, (Grand Rapids: Zondervan, 1958–59), VIII:314–15.
[2]Ibid., pp. 245–46.
[3]Ibid., VI:262–67.
[4]Charles Davis, *The Study of Theology* (London: Sheed and Ward, 1962), pp. 8, 10.
[5]Patrick Granfield, *Theologians at Work* (New York: Macmillan, 1967), p. 227.

CHAPTER ONE

[1]See Carl Bangs, *Arminius: A Study in the Dutch Reformation* (New York: Abingdon, 1971), 339–40. Arminius insisted that this privation makes depravity the necessary consequence; without the Holy Spirit the human spirit is corrupted.
[2]In a letter to me dated April 8, 1968.
[3]Robin Scroggs, "John Wesley as Biblical Scholar," *Journal of Bible and Religion* (October 1960), pp. 415–22. George Cell indicates that in selected parts studied, some one-half to three-fourths of Wesley's changes are paralleled in modern translations such as the RSV.
[4]Some said fifteen people went mad after Whitefield's first sermon. When Bishop Benson of Gloucester heard of this he remarked that he hoped the madness would continue.
[5]Rob L. Staples, "Sanctification and Selfhood: A Phenomenological Analysis of the Wesleyan Message," *Wesleyan Theological Journal* (Spring 1972).
[6]See Wesley's "Thoughts Upon Necessity," in Albert C. Outler, ed., *John Wesley* (New York: Oxford, 1964), pp. 474–91.
[7]Ibid., p. 489; see pp. 472–91.
[8]John Wesley, *Works*, (Grand Rapids: Zondervan, 1958–59), III:3–5.
[9]Peter Gay, *The Enlightenment* (New York: Knopf, 1966), p. 346.
[10]Edwin Newman, *A Civil Tongue* (New York: Bobbs-Merrill, 1975, 1976).
[11]John Wesley, *Journal*, ed. Nehemiah Curnock (London: Epworth, 1909–16), II:169.
[12]John Wesley, *Letters*, ed. John Telford (London: Epworth, 1931), VIII:230–31.
[13]See Derek Jarrett, *Britain: 1688–1815* (New York: St. Martins, 1965), p. 340. Richard Price, *Essay on the Population of England and Wales*, thought population had fallen by 25 percent in a century. Jarrett speaks too of the

enclosure acts (which Wesley protested), saying that from 1760–1800 there were some 1,900 enclosure acts affecting 3 million acres. By the middle of the century settled society was breaking up. There was large-scale migration to cotton towns of Lancashire, Cheshire, and Derbyshire. The old parish structure of static life (parish authorities prevented ingress or egress as much as possible) was changing. The landless laborer, who earlier in the century had been able to raise chickens and pigs, now had to fall back on poor relief.

[14]John Walsh, "Origins of the Evangelical Revival," in G. V. Bennett and J. D. Walsh, eds., *Essays in Modern English Church History* (New York: Oxford, 1966), pp. 140–42.

[15]E. Gordon Rupp, *Principalities and Powers* (London: Epworth, 1963), pp. 64–78.

CHAPTER TWO

[1]William R. Cannon, *The Theology of John Wesley*, (New York: Abingdon, 1946). Outler (in a personal note) judges this an incorrect understanding of Bull's *Harmonia Apostolica*. Robert Nelson's *Life of George Bull* takes great pains to deny that Bull was even close to Pelagianism, claims Outler.

[2]John Wesley, *Journal*, ed. Nehemiah Curnock (London: Epworth, 1911), IV:313.

[3]Ibid., II:275; John Wesley, *Works*, (Grand Rapids: Zondervan, 1958–59), VI:358–59.

[4]John Wesley, *Notes Upon the New Testament* (London: Epworth, 1966), pp. 862–63.

[5]Waldo Beach and H. Richard Niebuhr, *Christian Ethics: Sources of the Living Tradition* (New York: Ronald Press, 1955), p. 362.

[6]See *Journal*, II:15. When Wesley visited Germany in the summer of 1738, he was detained by the Duke of Weimar who asked why he was going to Herrnhut. Wesley responded, "To see the place where the Christians live." The hymn, which nearly repeats these lines was published at the conclusion of Wesley's "Earnest Appeal to Men of Reason and Religion," in the second edition, 1743. Later it was found in *Hymns and Sacred Poems*, 1749, "with Charles Wesley's name alone on the title-page." Curnock shows (p. 15, n.3) that Wesley was evidently influenced by an incident in the childhood of the mystic, Antoinette Bourignon when she asked her parents, "Where are the Christians! Let us go to the country where the Christians live." She is mentioned in Wesley's *Works*, IV:8 and XIII:127. For the text of the hymn, "Primitive Christianity," see *Works*, VIII:43–44. See Thorvald Kallstad, *John Wesley and the Bible: A Psychological Study* (Stockholm: Nya Bokforlags Aktiebolaget, 1974), pp. 145–50, for an analysis of Bourignon.

CHAPTER THREE

[1]The Wesleyan Methodists who moved away from the Methodist Episcopal Church in 1843, particularly in opposition to slavery.

[2]Luther Lee, *Elements of Theology*, or *An Exposition of the Divine Origin, Doctrines, Morals, and Institutions of Christianity* (Syracuse: Wesleyan Methodist Publishing House, 1856). Lee had been a professor at Adrian College, a Methodist Protestant institution.

[3]Ibid., 6th ed., p. 436.

[4]See Charles Jones, *Perfectionist Persuasion: The Holiness Movement and American Methodism, 1867–1936* (Metuchen, N.J.: Scarecrow, 1974). See my review of Jones's work in *Christian Scholar's Review*, 5:395–97.

[5]In conversation with a United Methodist bishop, sharing my continuing research in eighteenth- and nineteenth-century Methodism, the bishop indicated that Methodists are not especially interested in the Methodism of that era.

[6]Francis J. McConnell, *By the Way: An Autobiography* (New York: Abingdon, 1952); id., *John Wesley* (New York: Abingdon, 1939).

[7]Robert Chiles, *Theological Transition in American Methodism 1790–1935* (New York: Abingdon, 1965).

[8]Kathleen W. MacArthur, *The Economic Ethics of John Wesley* (New York: Abingdon, 1936). Robert M. Kingdon challenges this position in "Laissez-Faire or Government Control: A Problem for John Wesley," *Church History* (December 1957):351–52.

[9]Gerdes, Cooper, and Rogers wrote Ph.D. dissertations at Emory, Columbia, and Duke, respectively, in the sixties and seventies. The author of this essay wrote a dissertation on Wesley's views of church and state and a number of journal articles on Wesley's social ethics.

[10]Timothy L. Smith, "Doctrine of the Sanctifying Spirit: Charles G. Finney's Synthesis of Wesleyan and Covenant Theology," *Wesleyan Theological Journal* 13 (Spring 1978):92–113; "How John Fletcher Became the Theologian of Wesleyan Perfectionism," *WTJ* 15 (Spring 1980):68–87; "The Holy Spirit in the Hymns of the Wesleys," *WTJ* 16 (Fall 1981):20–47; "A Chronological List of Wesley's Sermons and Doctrinal Essays," *WTJ* 17 (Fall 1982):88–110.

[11]Donald W. Dayton, *Discovering an Evangelical Heritage*. (New York: Harper & Row, 1976).

[12]See his essays: "The Holiness and Pentecostal Churches: Emerging From Cultural Isolation," *Christian Century* (August 15–22, 1978):786–92; and, "Holiness Churches: A Significant Ethical Tradition," *Christian Century* (February 26, 1975):197–201.

[13]Earlier Wesleyan scholarship was largely nurtured at such evangelical schools as Northern Baptist Seminary, Gordon Divinity School, and the Biblical Seminary in New York.

[14]Ronald J. Sider, *Rich Christians in an Age of Hunger* (Downer's Grove: InterVarsity, 1977).

[15]Howard Snyder, *The Problem of Wineskins* (Downer's Grove: InterVarsity, 1975); id., *The Radical Wesley and Patterns of Church Renewal* (Downer's Grove: InterVarsity, 1980).

[16]Letha Scanzoni and Nancy Hardesty, *All We're Meant to Be: A Biblical Approach to Women's Liberation* (Waco: Word, 1974). Note discussion of Susannah Wesley on pp. 96–98, 188–90.

[17]The title of Jesse T. Peck's important book on sanctification, written in 1857 and reissued many times. See my "Reformation and Perfection: The Social Gospel of Bishop Peck," *Methodist History* (January 1978).

[18]See John Wesley, *Works*, (Grand Rapids: Zondervan, 1958–59) XI:1–164 for the major source of Wesley's ethics from the 1760s and beyond.

[19]Ibid., pp. 53–59; see "Thoughts on the Present Scarcity of Provisions" (1773).

[20]See Kingdon, pp. 351–52, where Wesley's double approach to poverty is discussed.

21Philip Watson, ed., *The Message of the Wesleys* (New York: Macmillan, 1964), p. 67, n. 75, claims that Wesley would have welcomed social legislation and the welfare state.

22See my essays, "War, the State, and the Christian Citizen in Wesley's Thought," *Religion in Life* (Summer 1976):204–19; "The Ethical Ministry of the Church: The Wesleyan Critique of Slavery," *The A. M. E. Zion Quarterly Review* (Winter 1976):219–29.

23See my essays, "John Wesley and Political Reality," *Methodist History* (October 1973):37–42; "Human Liberty as Divine Right: A Study in the Political Maturation of John Wesley," *Journal of Church and State* (Winter 1983):57–85.

24Jesse T. Peck, *The History of the Great Republic* (New York: Broughton and Wyman, 1869), pp. 679–80.

25This is not the same as the recognition that a particular state – e.g., Philistia or Persia–may be the instrument or "sword" God uses to punish evil.

26Helmut Thielicke, *Theological Ethics*, II (Philadelphia: Fortress, 1969):529–31, amplifies the problem for the state in handling conscientious objection, pointing out that it may function effectively only when objection is the exception.

27See my essays, "Pluralism, Toleration, and Evangelism," *Preacher's Magazine* (March–April 1978):14–16; "A Wesleyan Theology of Evangelism," *Wesleyan Theological Journal* (Fall 1982):26–42; "World Evangelization: A Wesleyan Proposal," *The Asbury Seminarian* (Summer 1982):18–38.

28Reformed scholarship remains nervous about Wesleyan theology, due in great measure to a general lack of understanding Wesley's doctrine of prevenient grace. Reformed thinkers are not convinced that the old free will-determinism debate has been won by the Arminians, as Geoffrey F. Nutall claims in "The Influence of Arminianism in England," in *Man's Faith and Freedom: The Theological Influence of Jacobus Arminius,* ed. Gerald O. McCulloh (New York: Abingdon, 1962), pp. 46–47.

29See the next chapter, "Creation and Grace."

30See my essay, "An Ethics of the Spirit: The Power and the Glory," *A.M.E. Zion Quarterly Review* (Summer 1976):94–107.

31In Romans 8; Colossians 1; Revelation 20–22. See also Wesley, *Works*, VI:157–66, 247–52, 288–96.

32Cf. Colin Williams, *John Wesley's Theology Today*, (New York: Abingdon, 1960), pp. 26–28. *Works*, VI:395.

33This phrase is Albert C. Outler's given in public discussion at World Methodist Historical Society, Toronto, Ontario, June 26–29, 1977.

34See Chapter six in this volume.

35Albert C. Outler, *The Christian Tradition and the Unity We Seek* (New York: Oxford, 1957), pp. 128–29. Dr. Outler says: "All the great Reformation watchwords-*sola Scriptura, sola fide, sola gratia*–have one essential meaning: *solus Christus . . . . Solus Christus* is the content of Christian theology and it is the source and center of Christian community." Cited in Robert McAfee Brown, *The Spirit of Protestantism* (New York: Oxford, 1961), p. 57.

36Wesley, *Works*, VIII:472.

37Ibid., XIV:321.

38Samuel Shoemaker, *With the Holy Spirit and with Fire* (Waco: Word, 1960), pp. 46–47.

39Eric C. Rust, "The Holy Spirit, Nature, and Man" *Review and Expositor* (Spring 1966):157–58.

[40]James H. Cone, *Black Theology and Black Power* (New York: Seabury, 1969), p. 57.

[41]John Macquarrie, *Paths in Spirituality* (New York: Harper & Row, 1972), pp. 42–47.

[42]See chapter 7 of this book, "An Ethics of the Spirit."

[43]Robin Scroggs, "Paul and the Eschatological Woman," *Journal of the American Academy of Religion* (September 1972):283–303. He affirms that Paul was a great spokesman for female equality, rather than a male chauvinist.

CHAPTER FOUR

[1]John Wesley, *Standard Sermons*, 5th annotated ed., edited by Edward H. Sugden, 2 vols. (London: Epworth, 1964), I:32.

[2]Ibid., pp. 33–34, emphases mine.

[3]*Religion and the Scientific Future* (New York: Harper & Row, 1970), cited by Charles Birch, "Participatory Evolution," *Journal of the American Academy of Religion* (June 1972), p. 148.

[4]F. J. McConnell, *John Wesley* (New York: Abingdon, 1939), p. 94.

[5]William R. Cannon, *The Theology of John Wesley* (New York: Abingdon, 1964), p. 179.

[6]Walter Brueggemann, "The Triumphalist Tendency in Exegetical History," *Journal of the American Academy of Religion* (December 1970), pp. 367–80.

[7]Cf. also his *In Man We Trust: The Neglected Side of Biblical Faith* (Richmond: John Knox, 1973).

[8]John Wesley, *Works*, 14 vols. (Grand Rapids: Zondervan, 1958–59), X:361–63.

[9]Ibid., VI:315, emphases mine.

[10]John Wesley, *Letters*, ed. John Telford, 8 vols. (London: Epworth, 1931), II:379.

[11]Wesley, *Works*, VIII:197–98.

[12]John Wesley, *A Survey of the Wisdom of God in Creation: or, A Compendium of Natural Philosophy*, ed. B. Mayo, 2 vols., 2nd ed., (Philadelphia: Jonathan Pounder, 1816), I:308.

[13]Wesley, *Works*, VI:213.

[14]Wesley, *A Survey of the Wisdom of God*, II:179–80.

[15]Erik Nordenskiold, *The History of Biology* (New York: Knopf, 1929), pp. 246–47.

[16]Robert Andrews Millikan, *Science and Life* (Boston: Pilgrim, 1924), pp. 48–50. In his *Explanatory Notes Upon the Old Testament* (Bristol: William Pine, 1765), Gen. 2:7, Wesley says, "Of the other creatures it is said, they were *created* and *made* but of man, that he was *formed* which denotes a gradual process in the work with great accuracy and exactness." Comparison of Wesley's comments with Matthew Henry's commentary on Genesis, which Wesley edited and enlarged to form his own commentary (particularly for the Book of Genesis), shows that Wesley took this idea directly from Henry. See *Matthew Henry's Commentary on the Whole Bible* (New York: Revell, n.d.), I:14.

[17]Wesley, *Works*, VI:213–14.

[18]Ibid., p. 249.

[19]John Wesley, *Notes Upon the New Testament* (London: Epworth, 1966), p. 991, note on Revelation 11:15.

[20]*Works*, VI:315–16, 338; VII:238–44.

[21]Ibid., VI:315–16, 338.

22Ibid., VII:170–71.

23Ibid., VII:228.

24Wesley, *Notes Upon the New Testament*, p. 303.

25Wesley, *Works*, VI:511.

26See Colin Williams, *John Wesley's Theology Today* (New York: Abingdon, 1960), pp. 45–56. In *Works*, VI:206, Wesley suggests that "honest Heathen" may be saved, "upon the plea of invincible ignorance." Wesley adds in one of his last sermons, "On Living Without God" (1790), that he cannot "conceive that any man living has a right to sentence all the heathen and Mahometan world to damnation. It is far better to leave them to Him . . . who is the God of the Heathen as well as the Christians, and who hateth nothing he hath made" (*Works*, VI:353).

27Wesley, *Standard Sermons*, II:41–47, emphases mine.

28Edward L. Long, Jr., *A Survey of Christian Ethics* (New York: Oxford, 1967), pp. 45–72.

29Wesley, *Standard Sermons*, II:49–50.

30See Wesley, *Works*, VI:247–52, for an exalted picture of God's new world (Sermon 60, "The General Deliverance").

31Ibid., XI:34, 37–38.

32Ibid., 70, 78–79.

33Wesley, *Notes Upon the New Testament*, p. 707.

34Wesley, *Works*, VII:513, 554.

35Wesley, *Works*, VI:288–96.

AN EXCURSUS ON CONSCIENCE

1Wesley, *Notes Upon the New Testament*, p. 303. In the sermon, "On Working Out Our Own Salvation," Wesley contends, "There is no man that is in a state of mere nature. . . . No man living is entirely destitute of what is vulgarly called *natural conscience*. But this is not natural: It is more properly termed, *preventing grace* . . . ." (*Works* VI:506–13). The same emphasis on the "graced" nature of conscience is found in the sermon "On Conscience."

2Wesley, *Notes*, p. 525.

3Ibid., p. 800.

4Wesley, *Works*, VII:186–94.

5See his essay on slavery in *Works*, XI. See my essay, "The Ethical Ministry of the Church: The Wesleyan Critique of Slavery," *AME Zion Quarterly Review* (Winter 1976):219–29.

6The phrase is from Peter Homan's *Theology After Freud* (Indianapolis: Bobbs-Merrill, 1970), p. 164.

7See my chapter, "The Concept of Conscience and Liberty of Conscience" in "Church and State in the Thought and Life of John Wesley" Unpublished Ph.D. dissertation, University of Iowa, 1971, especially pp. 192–209.

8Baxter's *Saints Rest*, Young's *Night Thoughts*, Thomas à Kempis's *Imitation of Christ*, Taylor's *Holy Living* and *Holy Dying*, Law's *Serious Call*, Allestree's *Whole Duty of Man*, Francke's *Nicodemus*, Annesley's *Exercise at Cripplegate* and Scupoli's *Spiritual Conflict* are some of the titles Wesley read.

9Francis Hutcheson, *An Essay on the Nature and Conduct of the Passions and Affections With Illustrations on the Moral Sense*, 3rd ed. (London: A. Ward, 1742). The work was first published in 1728 prior to his appointment as Professor of Moral Philosophy at Glasgow in 1730.

10Jean-Jacques Rousseau, *Emile* (London: J. M. Dent, 1911), pp. 244–58

[11]Edward H. Sugden, editor of Wesley's *Standard Sermons* 5th ed. (London: Epworth, 1961–64), pp. 44–45, believes that Wesley read Butler's sermons before 1788 when Wesley prepared the sermon on conscience.

[12]Joseph Butler, *Fifteen Sermons Upon Nature* (London, 1726) (my emphasis). See *The Classical Moralist*, ed. Benjamin Rand (Boston: Houghton-Mifflin, 1937), pp. 378–93, for the sources of Butler's comment.

[13]Wesley, *Journal*, V:492.

[14]Ibid., pp. 303–4. Hutcheson expanded Shaftesbury's notion of the "moral sense," an idea to which the latter gave little attention. Henry Sidgwick says that Shaftesbury is "the first moralist who distinctly takes psychological experience as the basis of ethics." Cited in *Characteristics*, ed. John M. Robertson (Indianapolis: Bobbs Merrill, 1964), p. xxviii.

[15]Hutcheson, pp. 4–5.

[16]Ibid., pp. 5–6.

[17]See Rand, pp. 395–417, for parts of the *Inquiry*.

[18]Hutcheson, pp. 286–89. Elsewhere he defines virtue as "agreeableness to this moral Sense," or "kind affection." The apprehension of good creates desire; evil, aversion (*ibid.*, pp. XV, 62).

[19]Ibid. p. 308. "There is in Mankind such a Disposition naturally, that they desire the Happiness of any known sensitive Nature. . . ." Wesley saw opposite indications (*Journal*, V:492–95).

[20]Hutcheson, pp. 334, 339.

[21]In his later years, Hutcheson used the term "conscience" interchangeably with "moral sense," a possible sign of Joseph Butler's influence. W. R. Scott, *Francis Hutcheson: His Life, Teaching and Position in the History of Philosophy* (London: Cambridge, 1900), pp. 198ff., esp. 199, 246. Hutcheson was a teacher of Adam Smith.

[22]Wesley, *Works*, VII:188–89.

[23]See Hutcheson, p. 333: "To be led by a weaker Motive, where a stronger is alike present to the Mind, to love a Creature more than God, or to have stronger Desires of doing what is grateful to Creatures than to God . . . would certainly argue great *Perversion of our Affections* . . . ."

[24]See H. Emil Brunner, *The Divine Imperative* (Philadelphia: Westminster, 1932), pp. 156 ff.

[25]Wesley, *Standard Sermons*, II:37–83. This sermon was probably prepared for publication during the antinomian controversy with the Moravians, about 1740.

[26]Wesley, *Works*, VII:190.

[27]Ronald Preston recognizes "an element of emotion in the workings of conscience because when the reason decides what *ought to be done* we feel emotionally drawn toward it, or emotionally divided if we partly shrink from it. See his "Conscience" in *Dictionary of Christian Ethics*, ed. John Macquarrie (Philadelphia: Westminster, 1967), p. 66.

[28]See Derek Jarrett, *Britain:1688–1815* (New York: St. Martin's, 1965), pp. 359–66 on "New Ways of Thinking." Jeremy Bentham's *The Principles of Morals and Legislation* echoes Locke, adding the necessity of legislation to insure "the greatest happiness of the greatest number." Locke's work was more specifically epistemological than ethical. Nevertheless, he argues that the principles of ethics are rationally intuited. Evidently, the mind's apprehension of right and wrong was related to the pleasant or unpleasant sense impressions that preceded the exercise of reason. Feeling is therefore crucial to the establishment

of a moral sense. In 1758, Claude Helvetius reduced all morality to various forms of a person's desire for pleasure or shrinking from pain.

[29]Leonard Krieger, *Kings and Philosophers:1689–1789* (New York: Norton, 1970), p. 166, credits Hutcheson with coining the phrase "the greatest good for the greatest number."

[30]Albert C. Outler claims that Wesley was a eudaemonist all his life. *Theology in the Wesleyan Spirit* (Nashville:Tidings, 1975), pp. 81ff. He cites fifty-four quotes from Wesley that pair off "happy and holy."

[31]Not to be compared with Freud's super-ego, which is the child's internalization of his parents' moral system.

[32]Wesley, *Works*, VIII:13.

[33]Wesley, *Works*, VI:353–55.

[34]Wesley, *Notes Upon the New Testament*, p. 609.

[35]Wesley, *Works* VII:191.

[36]Harvey Lewis, Jr., "A Theory of Conscience" *Spirit*, 3 (1979):19.

[37]See his comment concerning the human right to be wrong. (*Works*, VIII:125.) He cites Matthew Prior's poem, "Solomon on the Vanity in the World": "By force beasts act, and are by force restrained; The human mind by gentle means is gain'd: Thou canst not take what I refuse to yield, Nor reap the harvest, though thou spoilst the field."

[38]The longer Wesley's ethics is analyzed, the more one discovers a theological "system" for developing a serious social ethics. The stereotype of Wesley that sees all of his social concerns flowing from his warm heart ignores the fact that he was given to rational biblical religion as well as to experimental religion.

CHAPTER FIVE

[1]W. R. Cannon, *The Theology of John Wesley* (New York: Abingdon, 1946), p. 225.

[2]Wesley defined the "church" as a "company of faithful men where the pure Word of God is preached and the sacraments are rightly administered." See Wesley, *Works*, (Grand Rapids: Zondervan, 1958–59), VI:392 ff. When Bishop Butler said on the basis of hearsay, "I hear you administer the sacrament in your societies," Wesley responded, "My lord, I never did yet, and I believe I never shall." See Frank Baker, "John Wesley and Bishop Joseph Butler," *Proceedings of the Wesley Historical Society*, (May 1980), pp. 93–100.

[3]Wesley *Works*, VIII:270–71.

[4]Wesley will frequently ask the question: "Do you walk as He walks?" *Standard Sermons*, ed. Edward H. Sugden (London: Epworth, 1964), II:16. He will emphasize that serving God means "to *resemble* or *imitate* Him." Ibid., I:499.

[5]*The Christian Pattern, or a Treatise of the Imitation of Christ*, p. 1, cited in Cannon, pp. 56–57. Wesley translated the work in 1735, including it in his *Christian Library* under the title, *The Christian Pattern*.

[6]Wesley, *Standard Sermons*, I:313.

[7]Ibid., I:354–55.

[8]Ibid., I:313–77 for the three sermons on the Beatitudes. The quote above is from page 377, sec. 4, emphasis mine.

[9]Ibid., pp. 382–85.

[10]Ibid., p. 397.

[11]James Gustafson, *Theology and Christian Ethics* (Philadelphia: Pilgrim, 1974), 127–78.

[12]Wesley, *Standard Sermons*, I:431–32.

[13]In this passage, as Sugden notes, Wesley alters seven words and omits thirty others. See William Law, *A Serious Call to A Devout and Holy Life* (London: Epworth, 1961), pp. 29–30 and compare with Wesley's paraphrase in *Standard Sermons*, I:474–75.

[14]Wesley said: "You must be singular or be damned" (*Standard Sermons*, I:541).

[15]Ibid., 499.

[16]Ibid., 502.

[17]James Gustafson *Christ and the Moral Life* (Chicago: University of Chicago, 1976), 150–87. The author carefully discusses the various proponents of the imitation of Christ motif, addressing the question, "Which Jesus Christ is the ideal?" The Anabaptist tradition generally emphasizes the suffering Savior, although in some writings we see evidence of triumphalism—Christ the victor or Christ the king. To follow Christ is to suffer is the implication of accepting the former ideal, while reigning with Christ, here or hereafter, is the consequence of the latter. Clearly, the ideal to follow is the "whole Christ" but at that point comes the sincere moral man's cry of despair. At that point grace must intervene. Luther's statement, "Imitation does not make sons, but sonship makes imitators," reflects the priority of grace. See Lycurgus M. Starkey, Jr., *The Work of the Holy Spirit: A Study in Wesleyan Theology*, (New York: Abingdon, 1962), 108 n. Wesley certainly agreed with this position.

[18]This popular work (1896) is the effort of a Congregational pastor from Kansas. It asks the question: "What would Jesus do?" The book is part of the larger context of American liberalism. It is an optimistic portrayal of the possibility of imitating Christ. It has reputedly sold more than 8 million copies. Its weakness is in its lack of a realistic anthropology that emphasizes human inability to do what is known to be right.

[19]Wesley consistently teaches that Christian faith is made active in love or good works. He is concerned both with the outworking of faith in personal and social life. What makes the "good works" of the Christian good? Obviously not the intention in itself, but rather when the intention flows from faith. Nevertheless, the intention will be expressed in thoughts or actions. The process of execution is the point where even a "faithful intention" may be flawed, becoming what Wesley called an "involuntary transgression." Expressed differently, works that are rooted in faith are good works. When they are executed in specific life situations they may be good in actual consequence or not good, i.e., they may be harmful to oneself or to others even though good was intended.

[20]Gustafson, *Christ and the Moral Life*, p. 257.

[21]Ibid., p. 261.

CHAPTER SIX

[1]St. Augustine, *The City of God* (Edinburgh: John Grant, 1909), XIV:53.

[2]John Wesley, *Letters*, ed. John Telford (London: Epworth, 1931), VI:129.

[3]Olin A. Curtis, *The Christian Faith* (New York: Eaton and Mains, 1905), p. 373.

[4]Albert C. Knudson, *The Principles of Christian Ethics* (New York: Abingdon, 1943), p. 136.

[5]John Wesley, *Works* (Grand Rapids: Zondervan:1958–59), XIV:321.

[6]Ibid., VI:327–28.

[7]Ibid., V:485; VI:258, 260; VII:61; Wesley, *Letters*, III:35.

[8]R. E. Davies and E. G. Rupp, eds., *A History of the Methodist Church in Great Britain* (London: Epworth, 1965), I: xxxvi.

[9]It is necessary to show here that the context of Wesley's special concern was the quietism of certain of his associates who eventually separated from him, shaping Fetter Lane into a Moravian society.

[10]Albert C. Knudson, pp. 118, 138. See L. Harold DeWolf, *Responsible Freedom* (New York: Harper & Row, 1971), pp. 107–10.

[11]Wesley, *Works*, XI:415–16.

[12]J. G. Machen, *New Testament Greek for Beginners* (New York: Macmillan, 1948), p. 57; H. E. Dana and Julius R. Mantey, *A Manual Grammar of the Greek New Testament* (Toronto: Macmillan, 1955), p. 157.

[13]John Wesley, *Explanatory Notes Upon the New Testament* (London: The Epworth, 1966), p. 695.

[14]Francis Davison, ed., *The New Bible Commentary* (Grand Rapids: Eerdmans, 1953), p. 1011.

[15]Paul Althaus, *The Ethics of Martin Luther* (Philadelphia: Fortress, 1972) pp. 3, 10. See George W. Forell, *Faith Active in Love* (Minneapolis: Augsburg, 1954) for further discussion of Luther's ethics.

[16]*Supra.*, note 5 in this chapter.

[17]Quoted in Althaus, *Ethics,* p. 13.

[18]Wesley, *Standard Sermons*, II:77–78.

[19]James Gustafson, *Christ and the Moral Life* (New York: Harper & Row, 1968), p. 148. See chapter 3, "Christ the Sanctifier" and chapter 4, "Christ the Justifier." I have depended upon Gustafson's ideas for much of this discussion.

[20]Wesley, *Works*, V:462–64.

[21]Ibid., VIII:290.

[22]Wesley, *Notes Upon the New Testament*, pp. 862–63.

[23]Wesley *Works*, XI:417.

[24]Ibid., pp. 395–96.

[25]Gustafson, p. 118.

[26]Althaus, p. 13, n. 40.

[27]Daniel Benham, *Memoirs of James Hutton* (London: Hamilton, Adams, and Co., 1856), p. 112.

[28]Wesley, *Works*, VIII:290.

[29]Ibid., pp. 46–47.

[30]See particularly Wesley's statement from the 1759 Conference:

"Do you affirm, that this perfection excludes all infirmities, ignorance, and mistake?

"I continually affirm quite the contrary, and always have done so.

"But how can every thought, word, and work, be governed by pure love, and the man be subject at the same time to ignorance and mistake?

"I see no contradiction here: 'A man may be filled with pure love, and still be liable to mistake.' Indeed I do not expect to be freed from actual mistakes, till this mortal puts on immortality. I believe this to be a natural consequence of the soul's dwelling in flesh and blood. For we cannot now think at all, but by the mediation of those bodily organs which have suffered equally with the rest of our frame. And hence we cannot avoid sometimes thinking wrong, till this corruptible shall have put on incorruption.

"But we may carry this thought farther yet. A mistake in judgment may possibly occasion a mistake in practice. For instance: Mr. De Renty's mistake touching the nature of mortification, arising from prejudice of education, occasioned that practical mistake, his wearing an iron girdle. And a thousand such instances there may be, even in those who are in the highest state of grace. Yet, where every word and action springs from love, such a mistake is not properly a sin. However, it cannot bear the rigour of God's justice, but needs the atoning blood.

"What was the judgment of all our brethren who met at Bristol in August, 1758, on this head?

"It was expressed in these words: (1.) Every one may mistake as long as he lives. (2.) A mistake in opinion may occasion a mistake in practice. (3.) Every such mistake is a transgression of the perfect law. Therefore, (4.) Every such mistake, were it not for the blood of atonement, would expose to eternal damnation. (5.) It follows, that the most perfect have continual need of the merits of Christ, even for their actual transgressions, and may say for themselves, as well as for their brethren, 'Forgive us our trespasses.'

"This easily accounts for what might otherwise seem to be utterly unaccountable; namely, that those who are not offended when we speak of the highest degree of love, yet will not hear of living without sin. The reason is, they know all men are liable to mistake, and that in practice as well as in judgment. But they do not know, or do not observe, that this is not sin, if love is the sole principle of action.

"But still, if they live without sin, does not this exclude the necessity of a Mediator? At least, is it not plain that they stand no longer in need of Christ in his priestly office?

"Far from it. None feel their need of Christ like these; none so entirely depend upon him. For Christ does not give life to the soul separate from, but in and with, himself. Hence his works are equally true of all men, in whatsoever state of grace they are: 'As the branch cannot bear fruit of itself, except it abide in the vine; no more can ye, except ye abide in me: Without' (or separate from) 'me ye can do nothing.'

"In every state we need Christ in the following respects. (1.) Whatever grace we receive, it is a free gift from him. (2.) We receive it as his purchase, merely in consideration of the price he paid. (3.) We have this grace, not only from Christ, but in him. For our perfection is not like that of a tree, which flourishes by the sap derived from its own root, but, as was said before, like that of a branch which, united to the vine, bears fruit; but, severed from it, is dried up and withered. (4.) All our blessings, temporal, spiritual, and eternal, depend on his intercession for us, which is one branch of his priestly office, whereof therefore we have always equal need. (5.) The best of men still need Christ in his priestly office, to atone for their omissions, their short-comings, (as some not improperly speak,) their mistakes in judgment and practice, and their defects of various kinds. For these are all deviations from the perfect law, and consequently need an atonement. Yet that they are not properly sins, we apprehend may appear from the words of St. Paul, 'He that loveth, hath fulfilled the law; for love is the fulfilling of the law.' (Rom. xiii. 10.) Now, mistakes, and whatever infirmities necessarily flow from the corruptible state of the body, are no way contrary to love; nor therefore, in the Scripture sense, sin.

"To explain myself a little farther on this head: (1.) Not only sin, properly so called, (that is, a voluntary transgression of a known law,) but sin, improperly so called, (that is, an involuntary transgression of a divine law, known or unknown,) needs the atoning blood. (2.) I believe there is no such perfection in this life as excludes these involuntary transgressions which I apprehend to be naturally consequent on the ignorance and mistakes inseparable from mortality. (3.) Therefore *sinless perfection* is a phrase I never use, lest I should seem to contradict myself. (4.) I believe, a person filled with the love of God is still liable to these involuntary transgressions. (5.) Such transgressions you may call sins, if you please: I do not, for the reasons above-mentioned.

"What advice would you give to those that do, and those that do not, call them so?

"Let those that do not call them sins, never think that themselves or any other persons are in such a state as that they can stand before infinite justice without a Mediator. This must argue either the deepest ignorance, or the highest arrogance and presumption.

"Let those who do call them so, beware how they confound these defects with sins, properly so called.

"But how will they avoid it? How will these be distinguished from those, if they are all promiscuously called sins? I am much afraid, if we should allow any sins to be consistent with perfection, few would confine the idea to those defects concerning which only the assertion could be true.

"But how can a liableness to mistake consist with perfect love? Is not a person who is perfected in love every moment under its influence? And can any mistake flow from pure love?

"I answer, (1.) Many mistakes may consist with pure love; (2.) Some may accidentally flow from it: I mean, love itself may incline us to mistake. The pure love of our neighbour, springing from the love of God, thinketh no evil, believeth and hopeth all things. Now, this very temper, unsuspicious, ready to believe and hope the best of all men, may occasion our thinking some men better than they really are. Here then is a manifest mistake, accidentally flowing from pure love" (*Works*, XI:394–97).

[31]From the sermon, "You Are Accepted" in Paul Tillich, *The Shaking of the Foundations* (New York: Scribner, 1948) p. 162.

[32]Albert Outler, ed., *John Wesley* (New York: Oxford, 1964), p. 221.

[33]Carl Michalson, *Worldly Theology* (New York: Scribner, 1967), p. 134, writes that for Wesley, "There is a higher form of Christian existence than the life of faith and that is the life of works, which is 'faith working by love' . . . Faith is only the condition of or the means to works . . . Faith is instrumental to love."

[34]Wesley, *Standard Sermons*, II, pp. 455–56.

[35]Wesley, *Letters*, II, pp. 306–10.

[36]Wesley, *Works*, XIV:241 ff, 307–18.

[37]Ibid., p. 317.

[38]Cited in Outler, *John Wesley*, pp. 184–85.

CHAPTER SEVEN

[1]See Wesley's sermon on Matthew 5:13–16 in *Works*, (Grand Rapids: Zondervan, 1958–59), V:294–310

[2]Reprinted from *For Self Examination*, by Søren Kierkegaard, translated by Edna and Howard Hong, copyright 1940 and 1968, by Augsburg Publishing House. Used by permission.

[3]See Timothy Ware, *The Orthodox Church* (Baltimore: Penguin, 1963), pp. 218–23. Ware points out the recurring Eastern anxiety that the *filioque* dogma overemphasizes the unity of God at the expense of His triunity, and subordinates the Holy Spirit to the Son. Orthodoxy is troubled that the neglect

of the role of the Spirit in Western Christendom has contributed to the static institutionalism of Roman Catholic Christianity.

[4]Wesley's "Letter to a Roman Catholic" (July 18, 1749) emphasizes the equality of the Spirit, declaring that the Spirit is "infinite and eternal . . . ," ". . . perfectly holy in himself, . . . the immediate cause of all holiness in us; enlightening our understandings, rectifying our wills and affections, renewing our natures, . . . leading us in our actions; purifying and sanctifying our souls and bodies, to a full and eternal enjoyment of God" (*Works*, X:82).

[5]See H. Richard Niebuhr's perceptive essay, "Theological Unitarianisms," *Theology Today* (July 1983), p. 152. Niebuhr shows that unitarianism of the Spirit "looks to the reality found in the inner life rather than to the Being beyond nature or to the Redeemer in history for the fundamental principle of reality and value." It "absorbs the Creator and the Son into the Spirit . . . ," thus overcoming the otherness of God and the real physical presence of Jesus in history.

[6]Richard Lucien, "John Calvin and the Role of the Church in the Spiritual Life," *Journal of Ecumenical Studies* (Summer, 1974), p. 489, writes, "The Holy Spirit is God's personal presence among us in such a way that in the Spirit we attain God's own personal being."

[7]Wesley *Works*, X:82.

[8]In his commentary on Acts 2:1, Wesley describes the Pentecost of Sinai and the Pentecost of Jerusalem as "the two grand manifestations of God, the legal and the evangelical; the one from the mountain, and the other from heaven; the terrible and the merciful one." On Acts 2:38, he describes the gift of the Spirit to be "the constant fruits of faith, even righteousness, and peace, and joy in the Holy Ghost." See Wesley, *Notes Upon the New Testament*, pp. 396–401.

[9]Hendrikus Berkhof, *The Doctrine of the Holy Spirit* (Atlanta: Knox, 1976), pp. 88–89.

[10]Wesley, *Notes Upon the New Testament*, pp. 402, 411. In the course of his commentary on Galatians 5:20, Wesley declares that the works of the flesh include division and heresies. The latter is defined as "divisions in religious communities." This is Wesley's normal definition of heresy. Wesley also makes this point in his comments on 1 Corinthians 11:18; Titus 3:10; 2 Peter 2:1; and in *Works*, VI:404.

[11]See Wesley *Works*, V:294–310.

[12]John Wesley, *Standard Sermons*, ed. Edward H. Sugden, 5th ed. (London: Epworth, 1964), pp. 337–38. In the sermon, "On the Holy Spirit," preached on Pentecost 1736, the image and likeness of God is considered to be equivalent to the presence of the Spirit in Adam and Eve. In the Fall, Adam was found naked for "nothing less than God was departed from him." In consequence MAN is reduced to "that groveling life which is common to animals that never enjoyed the divine nature." However, to remedy the loss of the Holy Spirit, Christ "the Heavenly Word,—being a Spirit that issued from the Father, . . .—became MAN. . . . When he was incarnate and became man, he recapitulated in himself all generations of mankind, . . . that what we lost in Adam, even the image and likeness of God, we might receive in Jesus Christ." Christ, the "Second Adam" is, and was made to us, "a quickening spirit; by a strength from him as our Creator, we were at first *raised above ourselves;* [from the level of material creation to spiritual] by a strength from him as our Redeemer, we shall live again to God" (my emphasis). See *Works*, VIII, pp. 508–13. It is now understood that this sermon was from John Gambold, but that does not detract from its usefulness in understanding John Wesley, since it is incorporated in his

Works. See Timothy L. Smith, "A Chronological List of Wesley's Sermons and Doctrinal Essays," *Wesleyan Theological Journal,* 17 (Fall 1983):91.

[13]John Macquarrie, *Paths in Spirituality* (New York: Harper & Row, 1972), pp. 401–44.

[14]Cf. John H. Yoder, *Karl Barth and the Problem of War* (New York: Abingdon, 1970, pp. 18, 23–24. Here I use Barth's distinction between *ethos* and *ethics* : Ethos describes our manner of behavior, while ethics refers to the way we think about our behavior. With reference to the Spirit, ethos may be descriptive of His action, while ethics is thinking responsibly about His action.

[15]Wesley, *Notes Upon the New Testament,* pp. 2–3.

[16]Ibid., pp. 312.

[17]Nels Ferre *Christianity and Society* (New York: Harper, 1950), pp. 114–151, especially p. 136.

[18]Ibid., p. 135.

[19]Ibid., p. 133, 138.

[20]Wesley, *Works,* VIII:106.

[21]Ibid., pp. 102–5, where Wesley cites from twenty homilies to show the importance of the church's faith in the contemporary reality of the Holy Spirit.

[22]Ibid., p. 102. "In her Daily Service she teaches us all to beseech God 'to grant us his Holy Spirit, that these things may please him which we do at this present, and that the rest of our life may be pure and holy.' "

[23]Lycurgus M. Starkey, Jr., *The Work of the Holy Spirit: A Study in Wesleyan Theology* (New York: Abingdon, 1962), pp. 155–61.

[24]Carl Michalson, *Worldly Theology: The Hermeneutical Focus of An Historical Faith* (New York: Scribner, 1967), pp. 127–28.

[25]Wesley, *Works,* VIII:285–86.

[26]Cited in J. Ernest Rattenbury, *The Evangelical Doctrines of Charles Wesley's Hymns* (London: Epworth, 1941), p. 316.

[27]See Wesley, *Works,* XI:79 ("Thoughts Upon Slavery"), where Wesley makes a fervent plea for the liberty of the slaves, appealing to what this generation calls salvation history. In salvation history there is "a tendency to revive the past . . . in the service of paraenetic instruction." See Klaus Berger, "History of Salvation," in *Sacramentum Mundi,* ed. Karl Rahner, et. al. (New York: Herder and Herder, 1970), pp. 411–12. Wesley's attack on slavery appeals to such a principle as this.

[28]Bernard Ramm, *Rapping About the Spirit* (Waco: Word, 1974), pp. 68–69.

[29]See the comment from Nietzsche's *The Joyful Wisdom* cited in Heinz Zahrnt, *The Question of God: Protestant Theology in the 20th Century* (New York: Harcourt Brace Jovanovich, 1966), pp. 124ff.

[30]Wesley, *Standard Sermons,* I:268.

[31]Wesley, *Works,* VI:281–84. See sections 20 and 21 of the sermon. Wesley anticipates a future reprise of Pentecost, which will lead to the fellowship, sharing of possessions, care for the widows, and chaste conversation, which the early church knew. He repeats the Acts description of the dynamism of the church in the initial epoch of Pentecost, especially Acts 2–5. He further asserts that the Christian's words will be so "clothed with divine energy, attended with the demonstration of the Spirit and of power" that those who fear God (he mentions the "Mahometans") "will soon take knowledge of the Spirit whereby the Christians speak."

[32]A.S. Yates, *The Doctrine of Assurance,* (London: Epworth, 1952), p. 11, equates the Aldersgate experience when Wesley's heart was "strangely

warmed" with the witness of the Spirit. See my essay: "A Wesleyan Theology of Evangelism," *Wesleyan Theological Journal*, 17 (Fall 1982):36.

○ [33]H. Richard Niebuhr, *Christ and Culture* (New York: Harper, 1951), pp. 43, 190–229. See pp. 218–19 on Wesley as an example of a "conversionist."

[34]See George W. Forell, ed., *Christian Social Teachings* (New York: Doubleday, 1966), p. xi, for his typologies.

[35]See Hendrikus Berkhof, *The Doctrine of the Holy Spirit*, pp. 102–3, where the author stresses a pneumatological change in which the "age-old structures of man's life with their dehumanizing effects are replaced by the transforming powers of the Spirit."

[36]Paul Tillich, *Systematic Theology* (Chicago: University of Chicago, 1963), 3:111–12.

[37]By "Evangelicals" I mean such persons as Daniel Steele, Jesse Peck, Gilbert Haven, Randolph Foster, and many others who envisioned the progressive triumphs of Christ's gospel. Steele especially fought the proponents of a cataclysmic end to history ushered in by the Second Coming. See Daniel Steele, *A Substitute for Holiness: Or, Antinomianism Revived*, 3rd ed. (Chicago: The Christian Witness Co., 1887).

[38]Starkey, pp. 160–61.

[39]Daniel Migliore, "The 'Theology of Hope' in Perspective," *Princeton Seminary Bulletin* (Summer 1968), pp. 44–47. Teilhard de Chardin, *The Phenomenon of Man* (New York: Harper & Row, 1959), p. 229: "An animal may rush headlong down a blind alley or towards a precipice. Man will never take a step in a direction which he knows to be blocked."

[40]Mildred Wynkoop, *A Theology of Love* (Kansas City: Beacon Hill, 1972); and my "The Social Concerns of Wesley: Theological Foundations," *Christian Scholar's Review*, IV (1974):36–42.

[41]Macquarrie, *Paths in Spirituality*, pp. 50–52.

[42]See H. Richard Niebuhr, *Radical Monotheism and Western Culture* (New York: Harper & Row, 1960), for his interpretation of this concept.

[43]George Forell, "Luther and Conscience," *Bulletin of the Gettysburg Lutheran Theological Seminary* (Winter 1975), pp. 18–19.

CHAPTER EIGHT

[1]See François Wendel, *Calvin: The Origins and Development of His Religious Thought* (London: Collins, 1963), pp. 298–303.

[2]See Rupert E. Davies and E. Gordon Rupp, eds., *A History of the Methodist Church in Great Britain*, vol. 1 (London: Epworth, 1965), p. xxxvi. Reference to the second book of Homilies from 1563 shows the presence of three marks or notes: "Pure and sound doctrine; The sacraments ministered according to Christ's holy institution; and the right use of ecclesiastical discipline." See *Sermons of Homilies, Appointed to be read in Churches in the time of Queen Elizabeth* (London: Prayer Book and Homily Society, 1817), pp. 434–35.

[3]Emphasized in the evangelical creeds as a faith that saves, or, more specifically, justifying faith, to be distinguished from faith as assent.

[4]James Gustafson, *Christ and the Moral Life* (Chicago: University of Chicago, 1976), pp. 91–92.

[5]George F. Thomas, *Christian Ethics and Moral Philosophy* (New York: Scribner, 1955), pp. 213–16.

[6]See my essay: "Reformation and Perfection: The Social Gospel of Bishop Peck," *Methodist History* (January 1978), where this correlation of reform and holiness is studied.

[7]This revival has been emphasized by Albert Outler in his *John Wesley* (New York: Oxford, 1964), pp. 9–10; and V. H. H. Green, *The Young Mr. Wesley* (London: Edward Arnold, 1961), p. 260–61.

[8]John Wesley, *Letters*, ed. John Telford (London: Epworth, 1931), II:313–14.

[9]John Wesley, *Works* (Grand Rapids: Zondervan, 1958–59), VI:255ff.

[10]Ibid., 256–57.

[11]Even the first society of Christians at Rome had divisions, while Corinth has "not only Schisms and heresies, animosities, fierce and better contentions. . . , but open, actual sins . . ." (ibid., 258–59).

[12]Wesley's comments on Smyrna and Philadelphia in Revelation 2:9. "*I know thy affliction, and poverty*," are as follows: A poor prerogative in the eyes of the world! The angel of Philadelphia had in their sight but 'a little strength.' And yet these two were the most honourable of all in the eyes of the Lord." See his *Notes Upon the New Testament* (Rev. 2:9). Wesley was impressed by the corrupting influence of wealth, a theme often found in his writings.

[13]For discussion of Hooker and Pearson, see my thesis, "Church and State in the Thought and Life of John Wesley," (Unpublished Ph.D. thesis, University of Iowa, 1971), pp. 34–44.

[14]Wesley, *Works*, VIII:43–44. This hymn was inserted in the *Works* following Wesley's great apology, "An Earnest Appeal to Men of Reason and Religion," written c. 1744.

[15]A specific reference to Acts 4:32. Wesley concludes that this is the natural fruit of love. Of this sharing of possessions, he asserted, "It is impossible any one should [withhold his possessions] while all *were of one soul.* So long as that truly Christian love continued, they could not but *have all things common.*" On this practice of sharing, Wesley also claims that it should have "continued through all ages" if the prevailing community of love had endured. See his *Notes* (Acts 2:45; 4:32). Wesley, then, does not hold to the opinion that this community spirit was simply a response to a temporary need, i.e., the presence of many Christians in Jerusalem.

[16]Wesley frequently cited this stanza, e.g., in his *Notes* on Acts 2:42.

[17]The "remnant" concept of the church is also here. "The woman" is an obvious reference to Revelation 12:1–6. In his *Notes* on this passage, Wesley suggests that the woman is "the emblem of the Church of Christ," originating in Israel, enlarged by conversions, and finally the church in glory. The woman brings forth Christ, "considered not in His person but in His kingdom." Drawing upon Bengel, Wesley describes the "wilderness" as somewhere in Europe, "chiefly Bohemia" where the church was sheltered until the Reformation. It is not clear from whom or what the church is being sheltered, but apparently it is Satan. See John A. Bengel, *Gnomon on the New Testament* (Edinburgh: T. & T. Clark, 1860), V:258–86. See Sebastian Castellio, *Concerning Heretics*, ed. Roland Bainton (New York: Octagon, 1965), 49, 95, for the idea of the church as a remnant.

[18]Wesley, *Notes Upon the New Testament* (Acts 5:11).

[19]Wesley, *Works*, VI:395–96. E. J. Bicknell, *A Theological Introduction to the Thirty-Nine Articles of the Church of England*, 2nd ed. (London: Longman's, Green, and Company, 1925), 291–93, uses the term *coetus fidelium*. In Wesley's "Earnest Appeal to Men of Reason and Religion," he took the same position

many years earlier. The church is the "faithful people or true believers" (*Works,* VIII:35).

[20]*Works,* VIII:31. To support this argument Wesley immediately appeals to the Edwardian Reformation homilies written by Thomas Cranmer and others.

[21]Ibid., VI:395–96.

[22]Ibid.

[23]Roland Bainton, *Christendom* (New York: Harper & Row, 1966), II:118, describes the Pietist method, which emphasized Christian zeal and fervor whether among the orthodox or the heretics. Wesley's concern is that the believer reflect his new life in Christ even if his verbalization of the doctrine is deficient.

[24]Wesley, *Works,* X:80–86. Discussion of fundamental doctrines are seen in *Standard Sermons* , II:226–27. Cf. author's Ph.D. thesis, 276–90.

[25]A. C. Knudsen, *The Principles of Christian Ethics* (New York: Abingdon, 1943), pp. 237–38.

[26]Wesley, *Standard Sermons,* II:77–78. Wesley writes that "faith itself, . . . the faith of the operation of God, still is only the handmaid of love." In this sermon, "The Law Established by Faith," he views love as everlasting while faith lasts only as long as life.

[27]Not much evidence of a serious reading of Wesley is present. The last edition of his *Works* is a century old, but reprinted by Schmul (Salem, Ohio) and Baker (Grand Rapids), 1976–1979. Four volumes have appeared in the new Oxford University *Works* series, edited by Frank Baker.

[28]Albert Outler, "John Wesley as Theologian — Then and Now," *Methodist History* (July 1974), 81. Fortunately, there are tokens of hope. The Oxford Institute of Methodist Theological Studies met in 1977 to assess Wesley's contribution to liberation theology. It met again in 1982 in expanded discussions of Wesley's contributions. The Wesleyan Theological Society began in 1965 with 92 charter members. In 1981, the society reported 1,663 members. It publishes a semi-annual journal that focuses on Wesley's thought and its historical development.

[29]See H. Richard Niebuhr, *Christ and Culture* (New York: Harper & Brothers, 1951), pp. 32–39.

[30]*Prolepsis* is a technical term used in biblical studies to mean describing something future as though it were present.

[31]R. E. Chiles, *Theological Transition in American Methodism* 1790–1935 (New York: Abingdon, 1965), p. 122, and n. 25, where Chiles espouses a relational view of sin and salvation.

[32]Carl Bangs, *Arminius: A Study in the Dutch Reformation* (New York: Abingdon, 1971), pp. 339–40. Thomas N. Ralston, *Elements of Divinity* (New York: Abingdon-Cokesbury, 1924), pp. 140ff., follows Arminius more than Wesley, but in a synthesis suggests that sin is a *"depravation* resulting from a *deprivation."* Ralston says: "The scriptural view of the subject is, that Adam by sin forfeited the gift of the Holy Spirit from himself and his posterity, and this privation, as a necessary consequence, resulted in the loss of holiness, happiness, and every spiritual good. . . . It was only requisite for the Holy Spirit to be withdrawn, and moral evil, like a mighty torrent when the floodgate is lifted, deluged and overwhelmed the soul." Richard Watson is also cited as supporting this view. See Watson's *Theological Institutes,* (New York: Carlton and Porter, 1850), II:81–82.

[33]See the chapter on love, *supra.*

[34]Wesley, *Works,* XI:194–95

[35]Ibid., XIV:321. Preface to "List of Poetical Works" (1739). He calls such isolation "the grand engine of hell." Standard Sermons, I:381.

[36]R. G. Williams, "John Wesley's Doctrine of the Church" (Unpublished Ph.D. thesis, Boston University, 1964), p. 184. Cf. Wesley, Works, VI:255, 327; XIII:264.

[37]Wesley, Works, VI:327–38.

[38]Wesley, Standard Sermons, II:144ff.; I:378ff.; Wesley Works, VII:212–13.

[39]R. G. Williams, p. 180 ff.; Wesley, Works, VI:485; VI:258, 260; VII:61.

[40]Cf. Wesley, Works, VII:61; VI:258, 260, where Wesley speaks of a Christian society in Rome, Philadelphia, and Smyrna. Here he describes the church, even in spiritual decline, as a "Christian society."

[41]Wesley, Letters, III:35 (May, 1750).

[42]Wesley, Works, VII:60–62, 213.

[43]Ibid., XIV:321.

[44]Ibid., ". . .We should manifest our love by doing good unto all men. . . ." The Christian should "renounce any other or higher perfection than 'faith working by love'; 'faith zealous of good works'; 'faith as it hath opportunity,' doing good unto all men."

[45]Wesley, Standard Sermons I:382–85. Wesley sought for "social, open, active Christians" Ibid., p. 390.

[46]Ibid., p. 391; Works, X:68–69; Standard Sermons, II:77–80. "The Law Established Through Faith: II" (1749).

[47]Wesley, Standard Sermons, I:384ff.

[48]Davies and Rupp, xxxvi.

[49]Cf. Wesley, Standard Sermons, II:142, n. 1, where Sugden asserts that "Catholic Spirit" means "the spirit which regards as fellow Christians all who love the Lord Jesus."

[50]Ibid., II:134–35.

[51]Ibid., 144–45; I:397. "Royal law" probably means supreme law (James 2:8). Wesley's sermon, "The Good Steward" (1768), pp. 461–80, stresses the requirement of Christians to use all their capacities in mission.

[52]For these rules, see Works, VIII:269–75; XIII:266ff. Wesley's social theory has been interpreted in various ways. In The Message of the Wesleys, ed. Philip Watson (New York: Macmillan 1964), p. 67, Watson argues that Wesley would "thoroughly have approved the Welfare State," a postulate opposite to the individualism suggested in Donald B. Meyer, The Protestant Search for Political Realism, 1919–1941 (Berkeley and Los Angeles: University of California Press, 1960), p. 29. Meyer sees Wesley bypassing social needs and moving straight to the individual heart. Both are overdrawn, needing the balance of H. Richard Niebuhr, Christ and Culture (New York: Harper & Row, 1951), pp. 218–19. It is arguable that Wesley's social involvement rests on the concept of the church as a community of faith, expressing itself in love. His social theory rests upon the theological concepts of Christian society and Christian love. His sermon, "The Use of Money," calls for sharing on the basis of love.

CHAPTER NINE

[1]Maldwyn Edwards, John Wesley and the Eighteenth Century (New York: Abingdon, 1933).

[2]Wellman J. Warner, The Wesleyan Movement in the Industrial Revolution (London: Longmans, Green, and Co., 1930).

[3]Some lines of response may be indicated. First, the Halevy thesis is simplistic in its comparisons of the socio-religious context of England and France. Politically, England had already experienced significant advances in the seventeenth-century Petition of Right and Bill of Rights. Religiously, the Elizabethan *via media* had tempered the conflict between church and state, while the Act of Toleration had given dissenting bodies religious freedom to a significant degree. Second, one should recognize that the marvelously leveling influence of Wesley's message of "free grace for all men" raised thousands of men and women to a new life, which sharply changed their self-esteem. This revolutionized society by infusing into the national stream of consciousness a transforming vision. The following Methodist hymn from John Wesley, *Hymn Book* (London: William Reed, 1864), pp. 199–200, celebrates this revolution:

> For this, (no longer sons of night),
>   To thee our thankful hearts we give;
> To thee, who call'dst us into light
>   To thee we die, to thee we live,
>
> Suffice that for the season past
>   Hell's horrid language fill'd our tongues;
> We all thy words behind us cast,
>   And lewdly sang the drunkard's songs.
>
> But, O the power of grace divine!
>   In hymns we now our voices raise,
> Loudly in strange hosannas join,
>   And blasphemies are turn'd to praise.

[4]*Some Historical Account of Guinea* (Philadelphia: n.p., 1771). Comparison of the two tracts shows both Wesley's dependence and also his own thoughts. In Wesley's tract Section III, 8 is the beginning of his own comments. Benezet is more emotional, drawing pictures of suffering that excite sympathy. Wesley is more decisively ethical, presenting arguments that touch the conscience, motivate the will and call for decision.

[5]The "Crown rights of the Redeemer" is a Wesleyan motif, but is more conspicuously a part of Reformed ecclesiology. It is as ancient a concept as the New Testament. See J. S. Whale, *The Protestant Tradition* (Cambridge: The University Press, 1955), pp. 263–312, for discussion of the idea. Its primary focus is the claim of the Redeemer over against the claims of state or society.

[6]"Thoughts Upon Slavery" (1774), in Wesley, *Works*, XI:78.

[7]Lycurgus M. Starkey, Jr., *The Doctrine of the Holy Spirit: A Study in Wesleyan Theology* (New York: Abingdon, 1962), p. 162.

[8]Wesley *Hymn Book*, (London: William Reed, 1864), no. 447. Hymn no. 445, stanza one, is similar:

> O Come, thou Radiant Morning Star
>   Again in human darkness, shine!
> Arise resplendent from afar!
>   Assert thy royalty divine!
> Thy sway o'er all the earth maintain,
>   And now begin thy glorious reign.

Line 4 includes the concept of the "Crown rights of the Redeemer."

INDEX